WHAT IS CRITIQUE?
AND
THE CULTURE OF THE SELF

THE CHICAGO FOUCAULT PROJECT
*Arnold I. Davidson, Henri-Paul Fruchaud, and
Daniele Lorenzini, series editors*

The wide-ranging and groundbreaking works of Michel Foucault (1926–84) have transformed our understanding of the human sciences and shaped contemporary thought in philosophy, history, critical theory, and more. In recent years, the publication of his lectures, seminars, and public discussions has made it possible not only to understand the trajectory of his work, but also to clarify his central ideas and to provide a better overall perspective on his thought. The aim of the Chicago Foucault Project is to contribute to this enterprise by publishing definitive English-language editions of these texts and fostering an ongoing appreciation of the lasting value of Foucault's oeuvre in the English-speaking world.

Madness, Language, Literature
Edited by Henri-Paul Fruchaud, Daniele Lorenzini, and Judith Revel
Translated by Robert Bononno

*Speaking the Truth about Oneself:
Lectures at Victoria University, Toronto, 1982*
Edited by Henri-Paul Fruchaud and Daniele Lorenzini
English edition established by Daniel Louis Wyche

"Discourse and Truth" and "Parrēsia"
Edited by Henri-Paul Fruchaud and Daniele Lorenzini
Introduction by Frédéric Gros
English edition established by Nancy Luxon

*About the Beginning of the Hermeneutics of the Self:
Lectures at Dartmouth College, 1980*
Edited by Henri-Paul Fruchaud and Daniele Lorenzini
Introduction and critical apparatus by Laura Cremonesi, Arnold I. Davidson, Orazio Irrera, Daniele Lorenzini, and Martina Tazzioli
Translated by Graham Burchell

MICHEL FOUCAULT

WHAT IS CRITIQUE? *AND* THE CULTURE OF THE SELF

EDITED BY HENRI-PAUL FRUCHAUD,
DANIELE LORENZINI, AND
ARNOLD I. DAVIDSON

TRANSLATED BY CLARE O'FARRELL

The University of Chicago Press   Chicago and London

The University of Chicago Press, Chicago 60637
The University of Chicago Press, Ltd., London
© 2024 by The University of Chicago
Published 2024
Printed in the United States of America

33 32 31 30 29 28 27 26 25 24   1 2 3 4 5

ISBN-13: 978-0-226-38344-6 (cloth)
ISBN-13: 978-0-226-38358-3 (e-book)
DOI: https://doi.org/10.7208/chicago/9780226383583.001.0001

Qu'est-ce que la critique ? suivi de *La culture de soi*
Édition établie par Henri-Paul Fruchaud et Daniele Lorenzini
© Librairie Philosophique J. Vrin, Paris, 2015.
http://www.vrin.fr

Library of Congress Cataloging-in-Publication Data

Names: Foucault, Michel, 1926–1984, author. | Fruchaud, Henri-Paul, editor. | Lorenzini, Daniele, editor. | Davidson, Arnold I. (Arnold Ira), 1955– editor. | O'Farrell, Clare, translator. | Foucault, Michel, 1926–1984. Works. Selections (University of Chicago. Press). English.
Title: "What is critique?" and "The culture of the self" / Michel Foucault ; edited by Henri-Paul Fruchaud, Daniele Lorenzini, and Arnold I. Davidson ; translated by Clare O'Farrell.
Other titles: Lectures. Selections (2024). English
Description: Chicago : The University of Chicago Press, 2024. | Series: Chicago Foucault project | Includes bibliographical references and index.
Identifiers: LCCN 2023016772 | ISBN 9780226383446 (cloth) | ISBN 9780226383583 (ebook)
Subjects: LCSH: Criticism (Philosophy) | Critical theory. | Self (Philosophy)
Classification: LCC B2430.F722 E5 2024 | DDC 126—dc23/eng/20230424
LC record available at https://lccn.loc.gov/2023016772

♾ This paper meets the requirements of ANSI/NISO Z39.48-1992 (Permanence of Paper).

CONTENTS

EDITORS' NOTE *vii*

TRANSLATOR'S NOTE *ix*

ABBREVIATIONS OF WORKS BY
MICHEL FOUCAULT *xi*

INTRODUCTION *1*
Daniele Lorenzini and Arnold I. Davidson

WHAT IS CRITIQUE? *19*
Lecture to the Société française de Philosophie | May 27, 1978
Michel Foucault

THE CULTURE OF THE SELF *63*
Lecture at the University of California, Berkeley | April 12, 1983
Michel Foucault

DISCUSSION WITH THE
DEPARTMENT OF PHILOSOPHY *83*

DISCUSSION WITH THE
DEPARTMENT OF HISTORY *95*

DISCUSSION WITH THE
DEPARTMENT OF FRENCH *117*

NOTES *149*   INDEX *193*

EDITORS' NOTE

This volume presents two lectures by Michel Foucault: (1) a lecture delivered in French at the Sorbonne to the Société française de Philosophie on May 27, 1978, and published in 1990 under the title "Qu'est-ce que la critique? (Critique et *Aufklärung*)" and (2) a lecture delivered in English on April 12, 1983, at the University of California, Berkeley, titled "The Culture of the Self." In the days following this second lecture, Foucault took part in three discussions at Berkeley organized respectively by the departments of philosophy, history, and French. Transcriptions of these discussions—the first two in English and the third in French—can be found after the lecture in this volume. Five years separate these two lectures, a period during which Foucault's thought underwent significant evolution. Nonetheless, we thought it would be interesting to publish these two texts together. A few months prior to his lecture in April 1983, Foucault began his course at the Collège of France on *The Government of Self and Others*, with a long discussion on the Aufklärung, echoing the theme of his lecture to the Société française de Philosophie in May 1978.

The texts were prepared as follows:

For the 1978 lecture we consulted the transcript published in the *Bulletin de la Société française de Philosophie* 84, no. 2

(April–June 1990): 35–63. A number of changes were made to this transcript after viewing the manuscript held by the Bibliothèque nationale in France. These changes include (1) passages omitted by Foucault in his oral presentation and (2) variants from a first version of the transcript sent to Foucault for proofreading (a version that does not include his handwritten corrections).

For the lecture delivered at Berkeley on April 12, 1983, and for the three discussions that followed it, we consulted the recordings held by the University of California, Berkeley, and the Institut Mémoires de l'Édition Contemporaine (IMEC). Davey K. Tomlinson assisted with the English transcriptions. We were also able to consult the manuscript of the lecture at the Bibliothèque nationale in France.

The texts have been rendered as literally as possible. We have omitted some repetitions and hesitations when Foucault was searching for words, and we have corrected some incorrect sentences in the debates in English when it was essential. We have also taken the liberty of summarizing the questions in the debates and omitting certain exchanges that were off track. Editorial interventions are indicated with square brackets throughout the text. When the text of the spoken lectures differs significantly from Foucault's written manuscripts, the alternate text is provided in a footnote.

We would particularly like to thank the Bibliothèque nationale in France for their invaluable help and allowing us to consult documents in the Foucault collection that are not yet available to the public. We also thank the Société française de Philosophie for kindly authorizing the republication of the discussion which followed Michel Foucault's lecture on May 27, 1978.

Henri-Paul Fruchaud and Daniele Lorenzini

TRANSLATOR'S NOTE

I have provided references to existing English translations of works cited in the French edition. For references to works by Foucault that are collected in *Dits et Écrits*, I have included in parentheses the numeration used by these volumes to assist readers in cases where multiple English translations exist and for readers working in languages other than English. For items that have not been translated into English, I have provided the volume number and page from *Dits et Écrits*.

I have followed translation practices in other works by Foucault and translated Foucault's own words in his references to classical Greek and Roman literature. Passages of such literature in quotation marks in the lectures are usually paraphrases by Foucault, and any direct citations are to French translations or Foucault's own translations, which are sometimes quite different from the English translations of classical literature. I have consulted the digital Loeb Classical Library and a number of more recent English translations from the Greek and Latin for this English edition.

Clare O'Farrell

ABBREVIATIONS OF WORKS BY MICHEL FOUCAULT

AB   *Abnormal: Lectures at the Collège de France, 1974–1975*, ed.
V. Marchetti and A. Salomoni, trans. Graham Burchell, English series ed. Arnold I. Davidson (New York: Picador, 2003).

ABHS   *About the Beginning of the Hermeneutics of the Self: Lectures at Dartmouth College, 1980*, ed. Henri-Paul Fruchaud and Daniele Lorenzini, trans. Graham Burchell (Chicago: University of Chicago Press, 2016).

AK   *The Archaeology of Knowledge*, 2nd ed., trans. A. M. Sheridan Smith (London: Routledge, 2002).

CS   *The Care of the Self*, vol. 3 of *The History of Sexuality*, trans. Robert Hurley (London: Penguin, 1990).

CT   *The Courage of Truth: Lectures at the Collège de France, 1983–1984*, ed. Frédéric Gros, trans. Graham Burchell, English series ed. Arnold I. Davidson (New York and Basingstoke: Palgrave Macmillan, 2010).

DE I   *Dits et Écrits I, 1954–1975*, ed. Daniel Defert and François Ewald with the collaboration of Jacques Lagrange (Paris: Gallimard, 2001).

DE II   *Dits et Écrits II, 1976–1988*, ed. Daniel Defert and François Ewald with the collaboration of Jacques Lagrange (Paris: Gallimard, 2001).

DP   *Discipline and Punish: The Birth of the Prison*, trans. Alan Sheridan (London: Penguin, 1991).

EW 1 *The Essential Works of Foucault, 1954–1984*, vol. 1, *Ethics: Sub-jectivity and Truth*, ed. Paul Rabinow (New York: New Press, 1997).

EW 2 *The Essential Works of Foucault, 1954–1984*, vol. 2, *Aesthetics, Method, and Epistemology*, ed. James D. Faubion (New York: New Press, 1998).

EW 3 *The Essential Works of Foucault, 1954–1984*, vol. 3, *Power*, ed. James D. Faubion (New York: New Press, 2000).

FL *Foucault Live: Collected Interviews, 1961–1984*, ed. Sylvère Lotringer, trans. Lysa Hochroth and John Johnston (New York: Semiotext(e), 1996).

GL *On the Government of the Living: Lectures at the Collège de France, 1979–1980*, ed. Michel Senellart, trans. Graham Burchell, English series ed. Arnold I. Davidson (New York and Basingstoke: Palgrave Macmillan, 2014).

GSO *The Government of Self and Others: Lectures at the Collège de France, 1982–1983*, ed. Frédéric Gros, trans. Graham Burchell, English series ed. Arnold I. Davidson (New York and Basingstoke: Palgrave Macmillan, 2010).

HIST *The History of Sexuality*, vol. 1, *An Introduction*, trans. Robert Hurley (New York: Random House, 1978).

HS *The Hermeneutics of the Subject: Lectures at the Collège de France, 1981–1982*, ed. Frédéric Gros, trans. Graham Burchell, English series ed. Arnold I. Davidson (New York and Basingstoke: Palgrave Macmillan, 2005).

PP *Psychiatric Power: Lectures at the Collège de France, 1973–1974*, ed. Jacques Lagrange, trans. Graham Burchell, English series ed. Arnold I. Davidson (New York and Basingstoke: Palgrave Macmillan, 2010).

ST *Subjectivity and Truth: Lectures at the Collège de France, 1980–1981*. ed. Frédéric Gros, trans. Graham Burchell, English series ed. Arnold I. Davidson (New York and Basingstoke: Palgrave Macmillan, 2017).

STP *Security, Territory, Population: Lectures at the Collège de France, 1977–1978*, ed. Michel Senellart, trans. Graham Burchell,

English series ed. Arnold I. Davidson (New York and Basingstoke: Palgrave Macmillan, 2007).

UP *The Use of Pleasure*, vol. 2 of *The History of Sexuality*, trans. Robert Hurley (London: Penguin, 1985).

WDTT *Wrong-Doing, Truth-Telling: The Function of Avowal in Justice*, ed. Fabienne Brion and Bernard E. Harcourt, trans. Stephen W. Sawyer (Chicago: University of Chicago Press, 2014).

INTRODUCTION

Michel Foucault's thought underwent a series of transformations, but it always had the same recognizable style. The problem is how to capture both the modifications and this very particular philosophical style. Five years separate the two apparently distinct lectures that make up the heart of this volume. But there is at least one fundamental point of contact between them—namely, Foucault's engagement with Kant's text "Was ist Aufklärung?"[1] In both lectures, Foucault takes the opportunity to reflect on the scope of the Kantian critical enterprise while redefining it radically for his own purposes.

References to Kant's text recur in many of Foucault's writings between 1978 and 1984,[2] but they are usually brief, almost sporadic, without systematic analysis. There are two brief periods that are exceptions to this. First, in 1978, Foucault referred to Kant's text and the question of the Enlightenment, or Aufklärung, in his introduction to the American translation of Georges Canguilhem's *The Normal and the Pathological*.[3] Foucault then went on to deal with the Aufklärung at length in his lecture to the Société française de Philosophie. We are presenting the critical edition of this lecture here for the first time. Second, in 1983, Foucault dedicated the inaugural lecture of his course at the Collège de France *The Government of Self and Others* to Kant's text.[4] An extract from this lecture was published as an article in 1984.[5] Foucault then also published another essay on the topic in the United States that same year.[6] And in the lecture he delivered as part of the Regent's Lectures at the University of California, Berkeley, on April 12, 1983, Foucault also began with a brief discussion of Kant's text on the Enlightenment. His aim he says there was "to explain why I am interested in the theme of the culture of the self as a philosophical and historical question."[7] We are publishing this lecture here for the first time.

The two lectures we are presenting here, "What Is Critique?" and "The Culture of the Self," form two poles making it possible to examine the evolution of Foucault's thought between 1978 and 1983. They enable us to reflect on his different readings of "Was ist Aufklärung?" (a veritable toolbox in his hands) and also on the continuities that allow him to link his own historico-philosophical perspective and present and past work to the question of the "critique" introduced by Kant in his text on the Enlightenment. But, according to Foucault, this perspective cannot and should not be identified with Kant's own celebrated critical enterprise. Although the reference to Kant is pivotal for Foucault from the outset of his career in his supplementary thesis on *The Anthropology*,[8] Foucault highlights *another* Kant, or at the very least an alternative to the "Kantian" path of the *Critiques*, in an attempt to retrace the genealogy of his own philosophical practice.

An Indecent Title, or Kant versus Kant

The year 1978 was crucial in Foucault's intellectual trajectory. He introduced the theme of governmentality in his course at the Collège de France *Security, Territory, Population*.[9] This theme, in the form of the problem of the "government of oneself and others," was to make up the core of Foucault's research until 1984. In this course, while retracing the history of the idea and practice of government, Foucault alighted on what he termed "pastoral power" and offered a detailed study and analysis of five "pastoral counter-conducts" in the Middle Ages.[10] In addition, in January 1978,[11] in the introduction to the American translation of Canguilhem's *The Normal and the Pathological*, Foucault mentioned (albeit briefly) Kant's text on the Aufklärung for the first time. He emphasized the fundamental role played by Kant's work in postwar French thought, pondering the reasons for such a profound link between this type of reflection and the present. He argued that the history of science in France formed the context for the reactivation of the question of the Enlightenment as a way of examining "a reason whose autonomy of structures carries within itself the history of dogmatisms and despotisms."[12] The Enlightenment raised the question not just of the nature and basis of rational thought but also of its history and its geography, its past and its present existence. Thus, it was in first situating Canguilhem's work in the context of this kind of reflection that Foucault was able to describe the inauguration of a "philosophical journalism" at the end of the eighteenth century.[13] In proposing an analysis of the "present moment," this "philosophical journalism" opened up "a whole historico-critical dimension" to philosophy. Cavaillès, Koyré, Bachelard, and Canguilhem (as well as the philosophers of the Frankfurt School) all operated within this tradition.[14]

At the beginning of April 1978, Foucault left for a long trip to Japan.[15] During his stay he gave a series of important lectures,[16] and shortly after his return to France, on May 27,

1978, he delivered a lecture to the Société française de Philosophie. Several circumstances make this talk a real unicum in Foucault's intellectual production, beginning with the title. Indeed, Foucault begins by apologizing for not giving his lecture a title, explaining that the question he wanted to address was, What is critique? (This eventually did become the title when the text was published in the *Bulletin de la Société française de Philosophie* in 1990). However, Foucault admitted that there was a title that "haunted" him but that ultimately he didn't want, or even dare, to choose because it would have been "indecent."[17] This indecent title was of course "What Is Aufklärung?"—a title Foucault would no longer hesitate to use in 1984.[18] This leads one to wonder about the reasons for this hesitation, and the "game" that Foucault proposes to the members of the Société française de Philosophie.[19]

It probably has to do with the "torsion" that Foucault subjects the Kantian question of (transcendental) critique to, redirecting it toward what he describes as a "critical attitude." In fact, according to Foucault, if Kant did indeed transport the critical attitude and the question of the Aufklärung into the question of epistemological-transcendental critique, one now needs to go "down this route [...] in the opposite direction." This can be done by raising the question of the relation between knowledge and domination in terms of "a certain decisive will not to be governed."[20] In other words, just as in 1969 the seemingly classic question, What is an author? had been the pretext for making a (scandalous) shift from the author-subject to the author-function,[21] in 1978 the question, What is critique? opened up the possibility of making another (indecent) shift for Foucault. The epistemologico-transcendental question, What can I know? becomes here a "question of attitude,"[22] and critique is redefined as "the movement that allows the subject to take up the right to question the truth on its effects of power and to question power about its discourses of truth." The goal is "desubjectification in the play of [. . .] the politics of truth."[23] It is still in Kant, but in another Kant—the Kant of a "minor" and marginal text like "Was ist Aufklärung?"[24]—that Foucault finds the means to effect this shift. Now we can better understand perhaps what was so indecent about this gesture in a gathering of philosophers.

The Art of Not Being Governed Quite So Much

It should be noted, however, that it is not through a commentary on Kant's text on the Enlightenment that Foucault puts forward his definition of the critical attitude in 1978. This is why we must absolutely resist the temptation to read this lecture in the light of the 1983–84 texts. To do so would be to risk missing its threefold specificity.

First, the lecture to the Société française de Philosophie begins as an extension of Foucault's reflections in his course *Security, Territory, Population* rather than as a detailed analysis of "Was ist Aufklärung?" Foucault sets out to identify the emergence of a certain way of thinking, speaking, and acting that can be likened to a virtue he labels the "critical attitude." In his eyes, this emergence is linked to a historical phenomenon specific to the modern West—namely, the proliferation of the arts of governing from the fifteenth to sixteenth centuries onwards. This phenomenon testifies to the expansion into civil society of a form of power developed by the Catholic Church in its "pastoral" activity conducting the daily conduct of individuals.[25] So here Foucault is reworking more generally the analyses of "pastoral governmentality" he proposed three months earlier at the Collège de France.[26] But he puts forward a new thesis in "What Is Critique?"—namely, that the "governmentalization" that characterizes modern Western societies from the fifteenth to sixteenth centuries onwards cannot be dissociated from the question of "how not to be governed *like this*, by these people, in the name of these principles, in view of these particular goals and by means of these particular processes." The critical attitude thus receives its first definition without invoking Kant. A "general cultural form," a "moral and political attitude," a "way of thinking," it is both the companion and the adversary of the arts of governing—it is "the art of not being governed quite so much."[27]

At the Collège de France, Foucault focused on the points of resistance that had arisen within the Christian pastorate and offered a definition of "counter-conducts" in the Middle Ages. These were attitudes that demonstrated the will "to be conducted differently, by other leaders [*conducteurs*] and other shepherds, toward other objectives and forms of salvation and through other procedures and methods."[28] The proximity of this concept to the critical attitude as "the will not to be governed like this, by them, at this price" is obvious.[29] The "counter" and the "like this" testify to the always *local* and *strategic* dimension of these forms of resistance.[30] In fact, at the Société française de Philosophie, Foucault explicitly presents the study of pastoral counterconducts as a stage in the genealogy of the critical attitude.[31] The first "historical anchor" he mentions is the "return to scripture,"[32] and in the discussion after the lecture, he claims that the historical origin of the critical attitude should be sought precisely in the religious struggles of the second half of the Middle Ages.[33]

The second unique feature of "What Is Critique?" is Foucault's interpretation of the Aufklärung. Even if he situates the critical attitude within a history that is broader than just the "Kantian moment," rendering it "something other than the legacy of a particular stream of philosophical thought,"[34] he claims his definition of the critical attitude corresponds to the one Kant offered in 1784. This definition saw the Aufklärung as a courageous attempt to emerge from a state of minority imposed by an outside authority on humanity, rendering it unable to use its own understanding outside of a relationship of direction. In Foucault's reading, the Aufklärung becomes a practical attitude of resistance to a governmental power of direction. This exists within the field of relations between the subject, power, and truth—what Foucault calls the "source of critique,"[35]—and attempts to challenge, undo, or overthrow these relations. So, very clearly and much more explicitly than in his subsequent work,[36] Foucault pits the Aufklärung against epistemological critique, which is conceived by Kant as "prolegomena to all Aufklärung of the present and future." According to Kant, "it's less about what we undertake with more or less courage, than the idea we have of our knowledge [connaissance] and its limits and the implications for our freedom."[37] In other words, for Kant, the "courage in knowing" invoked by the Aufklärung consists in recognizing the limits of knowledge and gaining an autonomy that is not opposed to obedience, but on the contrary, constitutes its true foundation. Foucault goes on to assert that this critical enterprise that exists at a distance or "stands back" from the "courage of the Aufklärung" continued on into the nineteenth and twentieth centuries, in the form of the denunciation of the excesses of power that reason itself was historically responsible for.[38] Here, Foucault seems to want to distinguish himself clearly from this path, while still recognizing common points of interest with the Frankfurt School.[39]

The third feature that makes this lecture to the Société

française de Philosophie unique is the long methodological reflection in the final section.[40] Foucault returns here to the themes he dealt with a week earlier in a roundtable with historians,[41] and also to certain concepts he developed in the second half of the 1960s. He describes a "historico-philosophical" practice that seeks to explore the relationships between "the structures of rationality articulating true discourse and the mechanisms of subjugation linked to it." This practice entertains a special relationship with the Aufklärung, attempting to ascertain the conditions under which we can apply this "question of the Aufklärung—that is, the question of power relations, truth, and the subject—to any moment in history."[42] Redefined in this way, the question of the Aufklärung becomes the perspective Foucault uses to conduct his analyses and to rethink all his work.[43] The Aufklärung thus becomes a "trans-historical" question,[44] not just present in modern times (in the problem of the relation between reason and madness, illness and health, crime and law, etc.), but also within early Christianity and in Greco-Roman antiquity.[45]

But how precisely is this historico-philosophical analysis to be conducted? Foucault proposes a political approach to this question as a starting point in opposition to what he describes as an "investigation into the legitimacy of historical modes of knowing" that asks the question of the Aufklärung in terms of knowledge. He begins with the problem of power, advancing by using a "test by eventalization." On the one hand, it is a matter of avoiding the general question of truth and legitimacy as much as possible by substituting the terms "knowledge" (*savoir*) and "power" (*pouvoir*) for "fields of knowledge" (*connaissance*) and "domination" (with all their fixed limits).[46] The focus needs to be on "nexuses of knowledge-power" that are always specific and determined. Indeed, it is only by analyzing these nexuses, where the elements of power and the elements of knowledge are never dissociated, that it becomes possible to effect the passage from the empirical observability of a group of elements (the systems of mental illness, penality, delinquency, sexuality, etc.) to its historical acceptance. This is what Foucault describes as the archaeological level.[47] On the other hand, it needs to be demonstrated that these groups are not self-evident or necessary and are not enrolled in any transcendental a priori. This means analyzing these groups as "pure singularities," which must be seen as so many *effects*, without reducing them to "a unitary primary cause." Here we are at the genealogical level, which tries to restore "the conditions of the appearance of a singularity from multiple determining elements." It does this without ever operating a principle of closure, as the relations which make it possible to account for a singular effect display varying margins of uncertainty and a perpetual mobility. This is why this analysis is *strategic* in addition to being archaeological and genealogical.[48]

Approaching the question of the Aufklärung in this way (namely, in terms of the problem of the relationships between power, truth, and subject) means that power is not made to work as a fundamental datum or single principle of explanation. Instead, power is always considered "as a relation in a field of interactions" and associated "with a field of possibility and as such the subject of reversibility and possible reversal."[49] For Foucault, in other words, revisiting the question of the Aufklärung does not mean trying to understand how knowledge can form the right idea of itself, but rather highlighting the ethico-political value of an individual and collective *attitude* that consists in no longer wanting to be governed in a particular way. In 1978 (and in 1983–84) the analysis of Kant's text on the Enlightenment was therefore a way for Foucault to take stock of his own intellectual journey and assess the unique character of his work and its positioning in the field of contemporary philosophy.

The Aufklärung and the Historical Ontology of Ourselves

The question of critique and the Aufklärung appeared in several talks and texts in the following years without ever being the central focus. It then reemerged in a significant way in 1983, with Foucault deciding to devote the first lecture of his Collège de France course *The Government of Self and Others* to the discussion of "Was ist Aufklärung?" and, more concisely, of the second dissertation in *The Contest of the Faculties* (1798), where Kant asks the question, "What is the [French] Revolution?"[50] According to Foucault, these two texts testify to a specific way of philosophizing involving the interrogation of contemporary reality, an approach he argues was more or less inaugurated by Kant. Foucault does not emphasize this theme in his presentation to the Société française de Philosophie, but it is the most consistent element in his later series of texts and talks addressing Kant's article on the Enlightenment.[51] This is also the case in Foucault's lecture at the University of California, Berkeley, on April 12, 1983. Here, to explain why he is so interested in the theme of "the culture of the self," he begins by commenting on "Was ist Aufklärung?" emphasing that it was a "philosophical interrogation of the present," formulated in terms of a "very specific achievement" in the "general history of the way we use our reason." Foucault claims that Kant's text introduced "a new kind of question" into philosophy: it is not the question of how not to be governed in a particular way but of the historico-philosophical significance "of the precise moment when the philosopher is writing and of which he himself is a part."[52]

So in 1983, Foucault does not explicitly identify the question of Aufklärung with the critical attitude but with a different "historico-critical" question: What are we now? If he still locates a certain gap between "Was ist Aufklärung?" and the Kantian critical enterprise proper, he describes this gap in a new way. In this version, Kant inaugurated two irreducible philosophical traditions, even if these are linked in his own works. On the one hand, there is the tradition of the "formal ontology of truth" or the "critical analysis of knowledge" (What is truth? How is it possible to know the truth?). On the other, there is the tradition of "the historical ontology of ourselves" or "the critical history of thought" (What is our present reality? What are we as part of this present reality?).[53] Here, Foucault revisits the structure he had proposed a few months earlier at the Collège de France. This structure linked Kant's critical work to the tradition of "the analytic of truth," and his texts on the Aufklärung and the Revolution to a contrary critical tradition that raised the question of the "present field of possible experiences." Foucault called this "an ontology of the present, of present reality, an ontology of modernity, an ontology of ourselves."[54]

By asserting at Berkeley that he belongs to the second tradition, Foucault claims that "any ontological history of ourselves must analyze three sets of relations: our relations to truth, our relations to obligation, our relations to ourselves and others."[55] We recognize here the "source of critique" as Foucault defined it in 1978—namely, the relationships woven between subject, power, and truth.[56] In 1983, Foucault goes on to specify that while he had been led to primarily accentuate our relation to truth and power when he was studying madness, psychiatry, crime, and punishment, he now wants to study "the constitution of our experience of sexuality." He notes he is increasingly interested in our relationship with ourselves and "techniques of the self."[57] In volume 1 of *The History of Sexuality*, Foucault approached the sexual subject from the angle of its subjugation to a *scientia sexualis* and to the relations of power with which it was associated.[58] But it was in studying the experience of sexuality in Greco-Roman antiquity that he became aware of the crucial role played by the techniques of the self. These allowed one to form oneself autonomously (or at least partially) with respect to science and relations of power. Thus, in "The Culture of the Self," Foucault uses the discussion of Kant's text on the Enlightenment and of the historical ontology of ourselves to define the philosophical framework he claims to have always worked within.[59] This framework analyzes the relation to oneself and the techniques of the self that preside over the constitution of ourselves, and are also at the center of the "Greco-Latin culture of the self."[60]

The close link Foucault establishes between the study of "Was ist Aufklärung?" and his analyses of Greco-Roman antiquity is a distinctive feature of the Berkeley lecture when compared with his other texts and talks of the same period, where Foucault's discussion of "Was ist Aufklärung?" remained quite disconnected from his analyses of antiquity. This is with the exception of a lecture at the University of Vermont in October 1982, where Foucault maintained that the question formulated by Kant in his text on the Enlightenment (What are we now?) defines "the general framework" of the study of technologies of the self.[61] The "excursus" or "little epigraph" in the first lecture of *The Government of Self and Others* course,[62] marks a theme endowed with a perfect autonomy in the article published in 1984 in the United States.[63] It is only in "The Culture of the Self" that the reflection on Kant and the Aufklärung is tied in an explicit and structured way to the work that Foucault was undertaking on the texts of the ancient philosophers.

In wondering about the massive "return" of Kant's text in Foucault's talks in 1983, one is forced to recognize the close relationship between the critical attitude and the "courage of the Aufklärung," as Foucault defined these notions in 1978, and his study of ancient *parrēsia* as the courage of truth. Foucault was perfectly aware of this. Thus, in the last lecture of *The Government of Self and Others*, he argues that "Was ist Aufklärung?" is a way for philosophy to account for problems "which were traditionally problems of *parrēsia* in antiquity."[64] In the series of lectures he gave at the University of California, Berkeley, in the fall of 1983, he states that "by analyzing this notion of *parrēsia*" he wanted "to outline the genealogy of what we could call the critical attitude in our society."[65] It is probable that the "discovery" of *parrēsia* contributed to the increasing reflections on Kant and Aufklärung in Foucault's texts and lectures in 1983–84. But this link was not the only one, as "The Culture of the Self" demonstrates. Moreover, it is quite remarkable that, during the debate with the Department of French at the University of California, Berkeley, that took place shortly after this lecture, Foucault maintained that the same pastoral counterconducts he had presented in 1978 as the antecedents of the critical attitude also constituted a "reappearance of more autonomous forms" of the culture of the self in the Middle Ages.[66]

Cultures of the Self

The organization of the Berkeley lecture proves to be very close to Foucault's analyses published in *The Hermeneutics of the Subject*, particularly in his long summary of this course.[67] On the other hand, its structure is quite different from the second chapter of *The Care of the Self*, which bears the same title.[68] After the opening discussion on Kant's text on the Enlightenment, "The Culture of the Self" advances in three stages.

First, Foucault emphasizes the great historical importance of the principle of *epimeleia heautou* from Socrates to Gregory of Nyssa, explaining that in antiquity the rule and practice of knowing yourself were constantly associated and subordinated to the care of the self. This is why Foucault studies the *epimeleia heautou* in Greco-Roman culture as a "practical matrix for the experience of the self." Indeed, if "Greek metaphysics has determined our philosophical relationship to being," and if "Greek science has determined our rational relationship to the world," Greco-Roman culture has determined, according to Foucault, "our ethical relation to ourselves."[69] Foucault then proposes a close comparison between the form taken by this culture of the self in the fourth century BC and the first two centuries AD. Thus, in the Berkeley lecture, the expression "the culture of the self" does not just apply to the imperial period—where "the principle of care of oneself became rather general in scope," constituting a social practice and giving rise to the development of a genuine form of knowledge[70]—but also to classical Greece: "The culture of the self was not a late phenomenon in the wake of the decline of the classical city; it was an early phenomenon taking several forms in antiquity."[71]

In the second stage of his argument, Foucault analyzes Plato's *Alcibiades* as the first philosophical elaboration of the principle of *epimeleia heautou*. Summarizing the analyses in his course *The Hermeneutics of the Subject*,[72] Foucault emphasizes four points which, in his view, characterized the culture of the self in the fourth century. (1) The care of the self was linked to the political ambition of a young man who must first learn to care for himself in order to be able to govern the city. (2) The care of the self was linked to insufficient or defective pedagogy, one unable to teach the young man what he needed to carry out his project. (3) It was linked to an erotic and philosophical relationship between the young man and the teacher. And (4), the care of the self in the *Alcibiades* "takes the principal form of the soul's self-contemplation."[73]

In the third stage of his argument, Foucault describes the main features of the "new culture of the self" in the imperial era on the basis of this simple outline.[74] First, the relationship with oneself became permanent: taking care of oneself was no longer "a simple and momentary preparation for life; it [was] a form of life."[75] Second, the relation to oneself, which had become an adult practice, acquired new functions. These functions were as follows: a critical function (because you needed to get rid of bad habits, false opinions, and so on); a function of struggle (because the individual must be given "the weapons and courage that will enable him to fight his entire life"); a therapeutic function (philosophy being called on to cure diseases of the soul).[76] Third, the relationship with the master lost its erotic character and became a relationship of authority, a technical, administrative, and institutional relationship. Finally, fourth, the "new" culture of the self involved a widely varied set of techniques of the self, very different from pure contemplation of the soul.[77] (Foucault focuses in particular

on writing practices as techniques of the self at Berkeley.)
Thus, if it is indeed possible to speak of a "culture of the self"
in the fourth century BC, it was only during the imperial period that this culture was realized to its full extent.[78]

How is it, then, that the theme of the care of the self seems
to have "disappeared" in the modern and contemporary
world? Foucault provides several reasons for this. One reason
is the influence of Christianity, which formulated the care of
the self in terms of self-renunciation. Another reason is the
integration of techniques of the self into structures of authority and discipline, in such a way that the culture of the self lost
its autonomy. Further, there is the emergence of the human
sciences, which conceive of the relation to the self as a relation
of knowledge. And finally, there is the idea that the self is a
hidden reality that needs to be revealed or liberated.[79] But, as
Foucault explains in the debate with the Department of Philosophy, "the self is not a reality that is a given at the beginning
which must develop in accordance with a certain pattern or
model." Instead, the self *is constituted* "through a number of
practices, techniques which are characteristic of ethics." The
self is not a substance, but a set of relationships it establishes
with itself.[80] So, as he had done in his lectures *About the Beginning of the Hermeneutics of the Self*, where he had spoken of a
"politics of ourselves,"[81] Foucault concludes his lecture "The
Culture of the Self" by affirming that the self is nothing other
than "the correlative of technologies built and developed
throughout our history." The problem is not to free the self but
to consider "how it could be possible to elaborate new types
and new kinds of relationships to ourselves."[82] In other words,
for Foucault, restoring a historical and practical dimension
to the self does not mean, "bringing the whole weight of our

history down on our shoulders. Rather, it is to make available for the work that we can do on ourselves the largest possible share of what is presented to us as inaccessible."[83] This is one of the reasons why the space of reflexivity brought to light by the idea of "conducting *oneself*" turns out to be crucial to the way Foucault conceives the work of ethics.[84]

This historico-philosophical and ethico-political endeavor is explicitly linked to what Foucault called "the historical ontology of ourselves," drawing from "Was ist Aufklärung?" In this context, the question, Who are we? is not in fact a Cartesian question which is premised on "a unique but universal and unhistorical subject"—"Who am *I*? [...] *I*, for Descartes is everyone, anywhere, at any moment."[85] Instead, the question Kant is asking in his text on the Enlightenment is a Nietzschean question avant la lettre.[86] We are asking who we are *today*, "at this precise moment in which we are living," thus taking into account the contingent dimension of our form of the "self," and opening up the (theoretical and practical) possibility of "refus[ing] what we are."[87] It is about inventing new forms of the relationship to ourselves. Foucault concludes his article, published in 1984 in the United States, in a similar way: "The critical ontology of ourselves," he claims, "must be considered [...] as an attitude, an ethos, a philosophical life in which the critique of what we are is at one and the same time the historical analysis of the limits imposed on us and an experiment with the possibility of going beyond them [*de leur franchissement possible*]."[88] For all his interest in the Greco-Roman culture of the self as an aesthetic of existence, Foucault is not, in fact, proposing a return to ancient ethics as an "alternative" to contemporary moral models. Instead, he believes that this culture is in a position to show us the possibility of building a "new ethics," which, in the wake of the work of historical analysis tied to "the ethical imagination," bypasses the three major, and now weakened, references of religion, law, and science.[89]

Daniele Lorenzini and Arnold I. Davidson

WHAT IS CRITIQUE?

Lecture by Michel Foucault to the Société
française de Philosophie, May 27, 1978

HENRI GOUHIER: Ladies and gentlemen, first of all, I would like to thank Michel Foucault for making time for this session in his very busy schedule this year. We are catching him, I won't say the day after, but a couple of days after, a long trip to Japan.[1] This explains why the invitation sent out for this meeting was somewhat succinct. As Michel Foucault's paper is a surprise, and we can assume an agreeable surprise, I won't delay our pleasure in listening to it any longer.

MICHEL FOUCAULT: Thank you very much for inviting me to this meeting and to the society. I believe I gave a paper here about ten years ago titled "What Is an Author?"[2]

I haven't given a title to what I want to talk to you about today. M. Gouhier generously told you that this is because of my trip to Japan. In fact, he is very kindly stretching the truth. Let's just put it this way: I've been struggling to find a title the last few days; or rather, there was one that haunted me, but I didn't really want to use it. You are going to see why—it would have been quite indecent.

Actually, what I wanted to discuss, and still want to discuss, is, "What is critique?" I thought it might be worth trying to

say something about this project, a project that is constantly
being formed, extended, and reborn on the outer edges of
philosophy. It's a project that is close to philosophy, in close
contact with it, operating at its expense and headed toward
a future philosophy, perhaps even operating in place of any
possible philosophy. It seems to me that in the modern West
(dating roughly and empirically from the fifteenth to sixteenth
centuries) between the high-Kantian enterprise and the small-
scale polemical-professional activities which bear the name
of critique, there has been a certain way of thinking, saying,
and acting, a certain relationship to what exists, to what we
know, and to what we do, a relationship to society and culture,
a relationship to others as well, that we could call, let's say, a
critical attitude. You'll be surprised to hear, of course, that
there is something like a critical attitude that is quite specific
to modern civilization, especially when there have been so
many critiques and polemics and that even Kantian problems
probably have origins that stretch back much further than the
fifteenth and sixteenth centuries. You might also be surprised
to see a search for what unifies this critique, a thing that seems
doomed by nature, by function—I was going to say by profession—to dissipation, dependence, and pure heteronomy.
After all, critique exists only in relation to something other
than itself: it's an instrument, a means to a future or a truth
that it can never know and will never be. It offers a view over
a domain that it would like to police but where it cannot set
the rules. In short, it exercises a function subordinate to what
substantively makes up philosophy, science, politics, morality,
law, literature, and so on. At the same time, in spite of all the
pleasures and compensations that accompany this curious
activity of critique, it regularly—indeed almost always—
seems to carry with it a rigidity in the usefulness it claims to

have,* and also the underpinnings of a more general kind of imperative—even more general than the eradication of error. There is something in critique that can be likened to virtue. And in some ways, what I wanted to talk to you about was the critical attitude as virtue in general.†

There are many ways of embarking on the history of this critical attitude. I would like to suggest just one possible path among many. The variation I am proposing is as follows: The Christian pastoral or the Christian Church, insofar as it devel-

---

* Manuscript, instead of "rigidity": value.

† Manuscript: Between the high Kantian enterprise and small scale polemical-professional activities, I believe that in the West, there has been a way of thinking, saying, and doing that we could call the critical way. This has never been autonomous (and by definition never can be) and is always exercised within a field or in relation to a field—for example, philosophy, science, law, economics, or politics. Hence it is a scattered process but with interplays of relationships, connections, and relocations allowing these various activities to be articulated with each other, but the process is also specific enough for a certain style and common procedures to be easily recognized without too much difficulty in spite of this dissipation.

There is no owner or theoretician when it comes to critique. The universal and radical critic doesn't exist. The critic in himself and of himself doesn't exist. But in the West, every activity of reflection, form of analysis, or knowledge bears within itself the dimension of a possible critique. In any case, it is a dimension that is perceived as necessary, desirable, and useful; but it leaves one wanting, it's not sufficient in itself and as a result provokes mistrust and, as it happens, critique.

Beloved and despised critique, mocked mockery; its assaults are ceaselessly attacked by those it attacks, because all it does is attack and because its whole existence is about being attacked.

Impatience impatiently tolerated. What is this impatience that we see in the way of being and thinking in the West? Essential and precarious, fleeting and permanent.

What is this obligation that is constantly denigrated?

oped an activity that was precisely and specifically pastoral, developed the idea—I believe quite unique and also alien to ancient culture—that every individual, whatever his age or status, should be governed and allow himself to be governed, right down to the smallest detail of his actions, from the beginning right to the end of his life. In other words, he was to be directed toward his salvation by someone to whom he was bound in a global, yet at the same time meticulous and detailed, relationship of obedience.[3] And this operation of directing someone toward salvation in a relationship of obedience must take place in a triple relation to truth. First, truth understood as dogma. Then, truth where this direction implies a certain mode of particular and individualizing knowledge of individuals. Finally, truth understood as this direction deployed as a reflective technique which includes general rules, particular forms of knowledge, precepts, methods of examination, confession, discussion, and so on.[4] After all, we must not forget that for centuries what the Greek Church called *tekhnē tekhnōn*, and the Latin Church *ars artium*, was specifically the direction of conscience; it was the art of governing people.[5] Of course, for a long time, this art of governing was tied to relatively limited practices, even in medieval society, where it was linked to monastic existence and so shall we say practiced mainly in relatively small spiritual groups.* But I think that from the fifteenth century on, and also from before the Reformation, there was a veritable explosion in the art of governing people, an explosion that can be understood in two ways. First, we see a move away from its religious origins, a secular-

---

* Manuscript: It's true that it has recently lost much of its importance, complexity, and most particularly its autonomy in the wake of the human sciences.

ization if you like, and an expansion of the theme of the art of governing people and methods of doing this into civil society. Second, we see this art of governing being propagated into a variety of areas: how to govern children, the poor, and beggars; how to govern families and households; how to govern armies, different groups, cities, and states; also, how to govern one's own body and mind. In short: I believe "How do we govern?" was one of the most fundamental questions under consideration in the fifteenth to sixteenth centuries. This was a fundamental question to which the response was a proliferation of all the arts of governing—pedagogical arts, political arts, economic arts, if you will—and a proliferation of all the institutions of government, in the broad sense that the word "government" possessed at the time.[6]

Now, this governmentalization that I think characterized Western European societies in the sixteenth century cannot, it seems to me, be dissociated from the question of how *not* to be governed. I do *not* mean here that governmentalization was opposed in a kind of standoff with the opposite affirmation,* "We don't want to be governed, and we don't want to be governed *at all*." What I mean is that we find a perpetual question in this great anxiety about the way of governing and research into ways of governing. This question is how not to be governed *like this*, by these people, in the name of these principles, in view of these particular goals, and by means of these particular processes: not like this, not for this, not by them. If we bestow on this movement of the governmentalization of both individuals and society the historical integration and the magnitude that I think it had, we might be able to locate what could be called the critical attitude alongside it. Something

---

* Emphasis in original manuscript.

was born in Europe at the time that was both the opposite and a counterpart, or rather both a partner and adversary of the arts of governing. It was a way of being wary, challenging these arts, limiting them, finding the right balance, and transforming them, of seeking to escape from these arts of governing, or at any rate, displacing them through an essential reluctance. In addition, as part of the line of development of the arts of governing, a kind of general cultural form was born that was both a political and moral attitude: a way of thinking. I would call this quite simply the art of not being governed, or again the art of not being governed like this and at this price. Thus, I am proposing this general characterization as a primary definition of critique: the art of not being governed quite so much.[7]

You might tell me this definition is at once very general, really vague, and quite nebulous. It certainly is! But I still think it can provide a few specific anchor points for what I'm trying to describe as the critical attitude. These are historical anchor points,* of course, and could be pinned down as follows:

1) First anchor point: at a time when the government of people was essentially a spiritual art, or an essentially religious practice tied to the authority of a church and the magisterium of a scripture, not wanting to be governed specifically like this was essentially about finding a different relationship to scripture from the one linked to the functioning of the teaching of God.† Not wanting to be governed was a certain way of rejecting, challenging, and limiting (describe it any way you want) the ecclesi-

---

* Manuscript: Critique has a genealogy.
† Manuscript, instead of "the teaching of God": the religious institution.

astical magisterium. It was a return to scripture; it was
the question of what was authentic in scripture and what
was actually written in it. The question was: What kind
of truth does scripture utter, how do we access the truth
of scripture and in scripture, maybe in spite of what is
written? This, until we finally arrive at the very simple
question: Is scripture true? In short, from Wycliffe to
Pierre Bayle, scripture was in part, I believe, but not
exclusively so, crucial to the development of critique.
Let's say that critique is historically biblical.[8]

2) Not wanting to be governed is the second anchor point.
Not wanting to be governed in this particular way
is about not wanting to accept these particular laws,
because they are unjust, because behind their antiquity
or the somewhat threatening splendor bestowed on
them by the current sovereign, they conceal an essential
illegitimacy. From this perspective, critique confronts
government and the obedience it demands and opposes
it with universal and imprescriptible rights, to which all
government, whether monarch, magistrate, educator, or
father of a family must submit. In short, we are returning
to the problem of natural law.* Natural law is certainly
not a Renaissance invention, but from the sixteenth
century onwards it took on a critical function that it
has retained ever since. To the question, How not to be
governed? it responds by saying, What are the limits of
the right to govern? Let's say on this front, critique is
essentially legal.

3) Finally, and in brief, "not wanting to be governed" is of
course not accepting what an authority tells you to be

---

* Manuscript: Critique at its origins relates to nature.

true, or at least not accepting it just because an authority tells you it is true. You accept it only if you consider the reasons for accepting it to be good yourself. This time, critique anchors itself in the problem of certainty in the face of authority.

The Bible, the field of law [*le droit*], science; scripture, nature, the relationship to oneself: the magisterium, the rule of law [*la loi*], the authority of dogmatism. We can see how the interplay of governmentalization and critique has given rise to phenomena that are, I believe, of capital importance in the history of Western culture whether it involves the development of the philological sciences, the development of reflection, legal analysis, or methodological reflection. But most importantly, we can see that the source of critique can essentially be found in the range of relationships that bind power, truth, and the subject together in various ways.[9] If governmentalization is a movement that subjugates individuals through the reality of a social practice with mechanisms of power that claim to be based on truth, well, I would say that critique is the movement that enables the subject to take up the right to question truth on its effects of power and to question power about its discourses of truth. Critique is the art of voluntary insubordination, of considered indocility. Critique essentially performs the function of desubjectification in the play of what might, in a word,* be called the politics of truth.[10]

---

* Manuscript: This quick genealogy of the "critical way," and its location within the great process of governmentalization, has of course been done with the aim of resituating it within a broader history than simply the Kantian moment, making it something other than the legacy of a particular stream of philosophical thought. But it was also to link it to those elements of religious life that I think have marked it from the beginning:

Despite the character of this definition—empirical, approximate, and deliciously removed from the space it covers— I am arrogant enough to think that it is not so different from

- Critique as something that [challenges] governmentality (in either its general or particular forms) and its principles, methods, and results and raises the question of the salvation of each and all: whether salvation means eternal bliss or simply happiness.
- Critique as the suspension of the combined effects of power and truth, by the person who is subjected to it (I mean the subjugated element), this critique implies a decision on the part of the person who embarks on it. This decision is not something made in the background in relation to critical activity, a choice like a career or discipline, whose arbitrariness remains external to what has been chosen, but rather a permanent and definitive will even if it has the opportunity to reach its goal. It is an experience, in the full sense of the word, whether or not it is conducted as a first-person discourse or follows the path of deduction or empirical research. These things are important of course, but don't eliminate, make inroads into, or reduce the will to be critical as an individual decision-making attitude.
- The roots of critique in the history of Christian spirituality also explain why the critical attitude is not content to demonstrate and refute in general. It doesn't speak to everyone in general, it is addressed to each and all. It tries to establish a general consensus or in any case a community of scholars, scientists, and enlightened minds. It's not enough for it to say what it has to say for once and for all. It needs to be heard, to find allies, to have converts to its own conversion, to have followers. It works and battles. Or rather, its work is inseparable from a battle against two orders of things: on the one hand, an authority, a tradition, or an abuse of power; on the other, its complement—inertia, blindness, illusion, or cowardice. In short, it is against excess and for awakening.

In a word, critique is the attitude of challenging the government of people understood as the combined effects of truth and power, and this in the form of a battle which, starting as an individual decision, aims at salvation for all.

Kant's definition, not of critique but of something else. In the final analysis, it's not that far from his definition of the Aufklärung. In fact, it is significant that in his 1784 text on the Aufklärung,[11] Kant defined the Aufklärung as being a certain state of minority in which humanity is kept in its place in an authoritarian manner. Second, he defined and characterized this minority as a certain incapacity in which humanity was held, an incapacity to use its own understanding without precise direction by another. He uses *leiten* which has a well-defined historical religious meaning. Third, I think it is significant that Kant defined this incapacity as a certain correlation between an authority exercised to maintain humanity in this state of minority, a correlation between this excess of authority, and, on the other hand, something he considered and described as a lack of decision and courage.[12] Consequently, this definition of the Aufklärung is not going to be simply a kind of historical and speculative definition. There is something about this definition of the Aufklärung that is probably a bit ridiculous to call a sermon, but anyway, he certainly launches a call to courage in this description of the Aufklärung. We must not forget that it was a newspaper article. A study could be done on the relationship between philosophy and journalism from the end of the eighteenth century onwards . . . unless it has already been done, I'm not sure . . . It would be really interesting to see when philosophers began to contribute to newspapers on matters they found philosophically interesting but which also had a certain public appeal.[13] And finally, it is significant that Kant selects religion, law, and knowledge [*connaissance*] in this text on the Aufklärung as precise instances of where humanity is being maintained in minority—consequently as examples of instances where the Aufklärung must lift this state of minority and allow people, as it were, to come of age.[14]

What Kant described as the Aufklärung is what I was trying to describe before as critique, as this critical attitude that we see emerging as a specific attitude in the West originating, I think, in what was historically the broad process of the governmentalization of society. The Aufklärung's motto, as you know well and as Kant reminds us, is *"sapere aude,"* but not without the counterpoint of the voice of Frederick II: "Argue as much as you will and about what you will; only obey!"[15] In any case, how does Kant define critique in relation to this Aufklärung? I am not intending to recapture the Kantian critical project in all its philosophical rigor. Not being a philosopher myself and indeed barely a critic, I wouldn't take the liberty of doing so in front of this audience of philosophers. How do we situate *critique*, strictly speaking, in relation to this Aufklärung? If Kant effectively calls on the whole critical movement that preceded the "Aufklärung," how is he going to situate what he himself means by critique? I would say, and this is completely puerile, that in relation to the Aufklärung, critique in Kant's eyes is what says to knowledge [*savoir*], "Do you know how far you can know? Reason as much as you want, but do you know how far you can reason without danger?" In short, critique says that it's less about what we undertake with more or less courage than the idea we have of our knowledge [*connaissance*] and its limits and the implications for our freedom. As a result, instead of letting someone else tell you to "obey," it's only when you have formed the right idea of your own knowledge that you can discover the principle of autonomy and will no longer have to listen to the "obey"; or rather the "obey" will be based on autonomy itself.

I am not going to undertake a demonstration of the opposition between the analysis of the Aufklärung and the critical project in Kant. It would be easy, I think, to show that, for Kant himself, this true "courage in knowing" that was invoked by the Aufklärung,* this same courage of knowing consists in recognizing the limits of knowledge. It would also be easy to show that for Kant, autonomy is far from opposing obedience to sovereigns. But the fact remains in his enterprise of desubjectification in relation to mechanisms of power and truth that Kant fixed the essential task of critique as one of knowing knowledge [*connaître la connaissance*] as prolegomena to all Aufklärung of the present and future.†

I don't want to dwell on the implications of the gap between the Aufklärung and critique that Kant wanted to draw attention to. I would simply like to emphasize the historical aspect of the problem suggested by what occurred in the nineteenth century. The history of the nineteenth century provided many more occasions for the furtherance of the critical enterprise in light of Kant's location of this enterprise at a distance from the Aufklärung rather than in some way embodying the

---

* In quotation marks in the manuscript.

† Manuscript: The fact also remains that he derived the principle of dogmatism-despotism from the presumption of reason, its inability to remain within its limits and its naivety in forgetting its original determinations. In doing this, he introduced a hairline fracture, a split into the critical attitude, which means that the very thing allowing us not to be governed (or at least demarcating what it is to be governed) is perhaps what "governs us" inside without our knowing, making us fall into the heteronomy of despotism. What if we were governed without our knowing? What if what served us in the struggle against what governs us, condemned us to a kind of infinite governmentalization exercised in the name of reason?

Hence critique's step back from the Aufklärung, or, if you like, from the second critical standpoint in relation to the first. There is the naivety of the Aufklärung, whose unconsidered awareness paved the way for the extension and intensification of all the effects of despotism-dogmatism in the name of the natural rights of every reasonable subject.

Aufklärung itself. In other words, the history of the nineteenth century, and of course the history of the twentieth even more so, seem to have, if not proved Kant to be right, at least provided a concrete hold on the new critical attitude Kant opened the possibility for as an attitude that stands back from the Aufklärung.

This historical opportunity that seemed to be offered to Kantian critique far more than to the courage of the Aufklärung was embodied quite simply in three fundamental features. First, a positivist science, a science with a fundamental confidence in itself at the same time as it remained carefully critical of all its results. Second, the development of a state or state system that posited itself as the embodiment of reason and the profound rationality of history* choosing procedures of the rationalization of economy and society as instruments. From there to the third feature, the interlocking of scientific positivism and the development of states: a science of a state or statism, if you like. A network of close relations is woven between them, with science playing a more and more decisive role in the development of productive forces; and state-like powers being exercised more and more through collections of refined techniques. Following from this, the 1784 question, What is Aufklärung?—or rather the way Kant tried to situate his critical enterprise and his answer to this question—this questioning of the relations between Aufklärung and critique started to legitimately take on the appearance of mistrust, or in any case of a more and more suspicious interrogation. What excesses of power, what governmentalization, is reason not responsible for historically, all the more that the former seeks to justify its inescapability through reason?

---

*Manuscript: insofar as it is responsible for giving substance and autonomy to rationalities.

What became of this question, I think, was not quite the same in Germany and France for historical reasons that must be analyzed in their complexity.[16] Roughly you could say this: The suspicion that there was something in rationalization, and perhaps even in reason itself, that was responsible for the excesses of power had less to do with the recent development of a wonderful, brand new, and rational state in Germany than with the very old affiliation of the universities and Wissenschaft with administrative and state structures. It seems to me that this suspicion developed mostly in Germany, and let's say even more briefly it developed mainly in what might be called the German Left. In any case, from the Hegelian Left to the Frankfurt School, there was a whole critique of positivism, objectivism, rationalization, techne and technologization, a whole critique of the relationship between the fundamental project of science and technology, aiming to reveal the links between the naive presumption of science on the one hand and the forms of domination that characterize contemporary society on the other. To take as an example something that is probably the furthest from what might be called a leftist critique: We must not forget that in 1936 Husserl referred the contemporary crisis of European humanity to something that involved the relationship between knowledge and technique, the episteme and techne.[17]

In France, the conditions underlying the exercise of philosophy and political reflection were very different, and because of this a critique of a presumptuous reason and its specific effects of power doesn't seem to have been conducted in the same way.* I think we find this same historical indictment of

---

* Manuscript: except in a fringe of thinkers who remained isolated and marginalized.

reason and rationalization and the resulting effects of power within a certain segment of thought on the Right in the nineteenth and twentieth centuries. In any case, the block that made up the Enlightenment and the Revolution in general, probably prevented the real and profound questioning of this relationship between rationalization and power. Perhaps, in addition to this, there is the fact that the Reformation which, I think, at its deepest level, was the first movement of critique as the art of not being governed, didn't attain quite the same scale or level of success in France as it did in Germany. All of this meant that in France the notion of Aufklärung, with all the problems it posed, didn't take on such a broad significance and didn't become the same long-standing point of historical reference that it did in Germany. Let's say that in France people were happy with a certain political promotion of the eighteenth-century philosophes while relegating Enlightenment thought to a minor episode in the history of philosophy. But in Germany, what was understood by the Aufklärung was considered—whether for good or ill, it doesn't matter—as an important episode and a kind of brilliant manifestation of the profound destiny of Western reason. They tried to decipher, to recognize, the most salient fall line of Western reason in the Aufklärung and in this whole period from the sixteenth to the eighteenth century that serves as a reference point for this notion. At the same time the politics to which it was linked was the object of a suspicious examination. So, if you like, that is basically the chiasmus that characterizes the way the problem of Aufklärung was posed in France and Germany during the nineteenth and the first half of the twentieth centuries.

But I think the situation in France has changed in the last few years; and we have in fact reached a precise point where this problem of the Aufklärung (in the sense of its importance in German thought from Mendelssohn and Kant through to Hegel, Nietzsche, Husserl, the Frankfurt School, and so on) can be taken up in a rather meaningful parallel with, say, the work of the Frankfurt School. Once again, briefly, let's say— and this isn't surprising—phenomenology and the problems it has raised has brought us back to the question of what the Aufklärung is. Indeed this return has come to us through the question of meaning and what constitutes meaning. How does meaning come from nonmeaning? How does meaning come about? This is a question we can clearly see as complementary to another: How is it that the great movement of rationalization has led to so much sound and fury, and so much silence, and so many dreary mechanisms? We must not forget after all that *Nausea* and *The Crisis* are separated by only a few months.[18] Postwar analysis shows that meaning is only generated by the systems of constraint that characterize the signifying machinery. By a strange shortcut, it seems to me that once again we encounter the problem between ratio and power through the analysis of this fact that there is no meaning except through the effects of coercion specific to various structures. I also think (and a study probably needs to be done of this) that the analyses of the history of science, this whole problematization of the history of science (which is also probably rooted in phenomenology, and follows a whole other history in France through Cavaillès, Bachelard, and Georges Canguilhem), it seems to me that the historical problem of the historicity of the sciences echoes to a certain degree and demonstrates certain relationships and analogies to this problem of the constitution of meaning. How is this rationality born and formed from something quite different? Here we have the reciprocal and the inverse of the problem of Aufklärung: How is it that rationalization leads to the fury of power?

It seems to me that all this research into the formation of meaning, the discovery that meaning is established only through the structures of coercion of the signifier, as well as research that analyzes the history of scientific rationality and the effects of constraint tied to its institutionalization and model formation, it seems to me that all this historical research has done no more than throw a glimpse of daylight, through a kind of academic arrowslit as it were, on what was after all the fundamental movement underlying our history over the last century. After having it constantly drummed into us that our social or economic organization lacked rationality, we have found ourselves confronted with too much or too little reason— I don't know—in any case, definitely too much power. And after the constant singing of praises of the promises of the Revolution—and I don't know whether what it produced was good or bad—we were confronted by the inertia of a power that persisted indefinitely. And after hearing the constant recitation of the opposition between ideologies of violence and the real scientific theory of society, the proletariat and history, we found ourselves confronted with two forms of power that were like two peas in a pod: Fascism and Stalinism. Hence a return to the question, What is Aufklärung? This reactivates the series of problems that marked Max Weber's analyses: What are we to make of this rationalization that we agree has characterized not just Western thought and science since the sixteenth century but also social relations, state organizations, economic practices drilling right down to individual behavior perhaps? What are we to make of this rationalization and its effects of constraint and perhaps obnubilation, and its massive and growing implantation of a vast scientific and technical system that is never radically challenged?

We can approach this problem that we really need to shoulder responsibility for again in France—of just what is this Aufklärung?—in different ways. The way I'd like to approach this, and I would really like you to take my word for this, is absolutely not in a spirit of polemics or criticism. I hate polemics, and I'm really not very good at criticism.[19] So, two reasons why I'm only seeking to note differences and how far we can multiply, leverage, differentiate, and dislocate the forms of analysis that deal with this problem of the Aufklärung, something that is perhaps after all the entire problem of modern philosophy.

In tackling this problem, which shows our fellowship in France with the Frankfurt School,[20] I would like to note straightaway that setting up the Aufklärung as the central question necessarily implies a number of things. First, it means we are embarking on what we might call a certain historico-philosophical practice that has nothing to do with the philosophy of history or the history of philosophy. By this, I mean that the field of experience this philosophical work refers to does not exclude any other absolutely. It's not interior experience, it's not the fundamental structures of scientific knowledge, and it is not a collection of historical content elaborated elsewhere, prepared by historians and received as ready-made facts.[21] Historico-philosophical practice actually involves making one's own history, of *fabricating* it like fiction,* producing a history steeped in the question of the relations between the structures of rationality articulating true discourse and the mechanisms of subjugation linked to it.[22] We can see how this question shifts historical objects historians see as ordinary and familiar into the arena of the problem of the subject and truth, things historians are not concerned with. Likewise, we can see

* Emphasis in manuscript.

how this question invests philosophical work, thought, and analysis with the precise empirical contents it gives shape to. It follows, if you like, that historians faced with this historical and philosophical work will say, "Yes, yes, of course, maybe." In any case, the interference generated by this shift to the subject and the truth is never quite like that. Philosophers, even if they won't all react like startled guinea fowls, will generally think, "Even so, philosophy is something else entirely," which is due to the cascading effect produced by the return to an empiricity that does not even have the guarantee of an inner experience.

Let's grant these voices on the sidelines their full and considerable importance. They indicate, at least negatively, we are on the right track. We are asking a question through the elaboration of historical content to which we are tied because it is true or counts as true. The question is: What am I, this I, who belongs to this humanity, perhaps to this fringe, to this moment, to this instance of humanity that is subject to the power of truth in general and truths in particular? The primary characteristic of this historico-philosophical practice, if you like, involves desubjectifying the philosophical question by calling on historical content and liberating historical content by examining the effects of power as it affects the truth from which it is supposed to arise.* This historico-philosophical practice obviously also has a special relationship to a period that can be determined empirically. Even if it is relatively and necessarily vague, this period is, of course, designated as the moment modern humanity was formed—a period without fixed dates†—

* Manuscript: Let's put it this way: no fixed point, no apodictic [truth], no definitive result—a movement that just keeps moving.

† Manuscript, instead of "period without fixed dates": a period with flexible dates.

the Aufklärung, in the broad sense of the term used by Kant, Weber, and others. This period has multiple entry points as it can be simultaneously defined by the formation of capitalism, the constitution of the bourgeois world, the establishment of systems of state, the foundation of modern science with all its corresponding technical developments and also the organization of a face to face between the art of being governed and that of not being governed quite so much.[23] Consequently, this period is a real priority for historico-philosophical work, since visible transformations that are raw and on the surface appear there, relations between power, truth, and the subject that can be analyzed.[24] But it is a priority also in the sense that we can form a matrix for the trajectory of a whole series of other possible domains. Let's say, if you like, the problem of the Aufklärung isn't simply making an appearance because of my interest in and prioritization of the eighteenth century. Rather, I would say, basically it is my interest in posing the problem of what the Aufklärung is that allows the historical schema of our modernity to be unearthed.* It is not about saying that the fifth-century Greeks were a bit like the eighteenth-century philosophes or that the twelfth century was already a kind of Renaissance. Instead, the point is to try and see what conditions, modifications, and generalizations are needed to allow the application of this question of the Aufklärung—that is, the question of power relations, truth, and the subject—to any moment in history.

This is the general framework of the research I am describing as historico-philosophical. How do we go on to carry it out?

In any case, as I said earlier, I wanted to sketch a very general outline of possible paths other than those that seem the most

---

* Manuscript, instead of "schema": threshold.

well trodden to date. This is not to accuse them of leading no-
where, or not delivering valuable results. I simply wanted to
say this and suggest that the question of the Aufklärung since
Kant, because of Kant, and probably because of the gap he introduced between the Aufklärung and critique was essentially
raised in terms of knowledge [*connaissance*], or what became
the historical destiny of knowledge when modern science was
established. The question was also raised by looking for what
already marked the undefined effects of power in this destiny
to which it would necessarily be bound by objectivism, positivism, technicism, and so on. In relating this knowledge to
the conditions of the formation and legitimacy of all possible
knowledge, and finally by seeking how the passage away from
legitimacy (illusion, error, forgetting, recovery, and so on)
took place historically. In brief, it is a process of analysis that I
think was basically set in motion by the mismatch between critique and the Aufklärung instigated by Kant. I think from that
moment on, there was a process of analysis, and basically the
one that's most often followed, that could be described as an
inquiry into the legitimacy of historical modes of knowing. In
any case, this is how a certain number of eighteenth-century
philosophers, and how Dilthey, Habermas, and others have
understood it. To put it even more simply: What false idea
did knowledge have of itself and to what excessive uses was
it exposed, and what domination was it linked to as a consequence?*

Well, we might perhaps envisage a process other than the
form of an inquiry into the legitimacy of historical modes
of knowing. It could take the problem of power rather than

---

*Manuscript: This is indeed the implementation of the Kantian
question.

knowledge [*connaissance*] as an entry point into the question of the Aufklärung. Rather than an inquiry into legitimacy, it could advance as something that I might call a test by *eventalization*.[25] Forgive me for this dreadful word! Let's discuss what that means. Should historians be exclaiming in horror at this point, what I understand by the process of eventalization is this: First, we can take groups of elements where we can immediately identify connections between mechanisms of coercion and bodies of knowledge in a completely empirical and provisional way. This includes various mechanisms of coercion, maybe bodies of legislation as well, regulations, material devices [*dispositifs*], manifestations of authority, and so on. Knowledge contents also need to be taken into account in their diversity and heterogeneity and viewed in the context of the effects of power they embody in the process of their validation as part of a system of knowledge. It's not a matter of trying to determine what's true or false, founded or unfounded, real or illusory, scientific or ideological, legitimate or unjustified. We are trying to find what links and connections between mechanisms of coercion and elements of knowledge can be identified and what interplays of reflection and reinforcement develop between these aspects. This means that a given element of knowledge might take on the effects of power assigned in a given system to an element that is true, probable, uncertain, or false. The result is that a particular process of coercion may take on the form and justifications that characterize a rational, calculated, and technically efficient element, and so on.

So at this first level, the idea is not to engage in deciding legitimacy, or assigning the point of error or illusion.* And this

---

* Manuscript: the limit of excess or abuse.

is why, at this level, I think we can use two words whose function is not to designate entities, forces [*puissances*], or things like transcendentals. Their function is to operate instead a systematic reduction of value in a given domain, let's say a neutralization of legitimacy effects, highlighting what makes them acceptable and accepted at a certain moment in time. Thus the use of the word "knowledge" [*savoir*] to refer to all the processes and effects of knowledge practices [*connaissance*] that are acceptable at a given time and in a particular domain. The second term is "power" [*pouvoir*], which simply covers a whole series of specific definable and defined mechanisms able to induce behavior or discourse. We can see right away that these two terms have nothing but a methodological role. These terms can't be used to identify the general principles of reality; rather, they serve to fix the frontline of analysis and the relevant type of element for analysis. So right from the outset, we can avoid the prospect of legitimation the terms "field of knowledge" [*connaissance*][26] and "domination" put into play.[27] At each point in the analysis we also need to be able to give each element of knowlege [*savoir*] or mechanism of power [*pouvoir*] a specific and precise content. We must never posit the existence of *a* knowledge or, worse still, *a* power—that is, knowledge with a capital *K* or power with a capital *P* both operating in their own right. Knowledge and power can only function as an analytical framework. And as you can see, the two categories of elements in this framework are certainly not strangers to each other with knowledge off to one side and power off to the other. What I was saying about them earlier made them external to each other. Nothing can figure as an element of knowledge if it does not obey a particular set of rules and constraints—for example, the rules of a particular type of scientific discourse in a given era. Neither can it function as knowledge if it is not equipped with effects of coercion or simply the incentives specific to its validity as scientific, simply rational, or common sense. Conversely, nothing can function as a mechanism of power if it does not deploy according to the processes, instruments, means, and objectives validated by reasonably coherent systems of knowledge.[28] So it's not a matter of describing what knowledge is or what power is and how one might repress or abuse the other. Rather it's about describing a nexus of knowledge-power [*savoir-pouvoir*] with a view to understanding what makes a system acceptable, whether it's the system of mental illness, penality, delinquency, or sexuality, and so on.

In short, I think the path from the empirical observability for us of a situation to its historical acceptability at the time it was actually observable goes by way of an analysis of the underlying nexus of knowledge-power, recapturing it at the point it was accepted. This then takes us in the direction of what makes it acceptable, not in general of course but only in that instance when it was accepted. This is what we might characterize as recapturing it in its positivity.[29] So here we have a type of procedure that analyzes the cycle of positivity from the instance of its acceptance to the system of acceptability from the perspective of the interplay of knowledge-power. This happens beyond any concern for legitimation, consequently sidelining the fundamental point of view of the law. Let's say roughly this is the *archaeological* level.[30]

Second, it is immediately apparent that this type of analysis poses a certain number of dangers that cannot fail to appear as the negative and costly consequences of such an analysis.

These positivities are not self-evident entities in the sense that they have not been rendered acceptable by some originary law, no matter what habit or routine has made them familiar, no matter what blinding forces and justifications mechanisms of power have exerted and elaborated. It is important to emphasize that what made these positivities acceptable was not self-evident, they were not inscribed in any a priori or included in any anteriority. Disentangling the conditions of what makes a system acceptable and following the lines of rupture that mark its emergence are two related operations. It was not at all self-evident that madness and mental illness were superimposed in the institutional and scientific system of psychiatry. It was no more of a given that punitive procedures, imprisonment, and penitentiary discipline came to be articulated in a penal system; neither was it a given that desire, concupiscence, and the sexual behavior of individuals came to be effectively articulated with each other in a system of knowledge and normality called sexuality. The identification of what makes a system acceptable is inseparable from the identification of what makes it difficult to accept: its arbitrariness in terms of systems of knowledge [*connaissance*], its violence in terms of power, in short its energy.* Hence the necessity to deal with this structure in order to pay better attention to its ruses.

The second consequence, which is also costly and negative, is that these structures are not analyzed as universals to which the particularities and circumstances of history bring a certain number of modifications. Of course, many accepted elements and the conditions that make them acceptable may well have a long career behind them; but we need to recapture what are in a way the pure singularities in the analysis of these positivities.[31] These singularities are not the incarnation of an essence or the individualization of a species. Take, for instance, that singularity which is madness in the modern Western world,

---

* Manuscript, instead of "its energy": its emergence.

the absolute singularity of sexuality or the absolute singularity that is the juridico-moral system of our punishments.

There can be no appeal to a founding instance, no escape into a pure form, and this is probably one of the most significant and contestable points of this historico-philosophical approach. If it's not to slide into a philosophy of history or a historical analysis, it must remain in the field of immanence of pure singularities. So what comes next? Break, discontinuity, singularity, pure description, a motionless tableau, no explanation, a dead end, you know all that. You might say that the analysis of these positivities doesn't belong to the so-called explanatory procedures which attribute a causal value in accordance with the following three conditions:

1) Causal values are only recognized for explanations which set up one final instance and only one, an instance that is valorized as profoundly important: the economy for some and demography for others.

2) Causal value is only recognized for things that conform to a pyramidalization pointing to "the" cause or the causal source and unitary point of origin.

3) And finally, causal value is only recognized in what establishes a certain inevitability or at least something that approaches necessity.

The analysis of positivities, insofar as it concerns pure singularities that do not refer either to a species or an essence but to simple conditions that make something acceptable, well, this analysis assumes the deployment of a complex and tightly knit causal network that is probably of a different kind. It is a causal network that quite specifically doesn't require saturation by a deep, unitary, pyramidalizing, and necessitating principle.

It's a matter of establishing a network that accounts for this singularity as an effect—hence the necessity of a multiplicity of relations and differentiation between different forms of relations, differentiation between different forms of necessity in connections, the deciphering of interactions and circular actions, and taking into account the intersection of heterogeneous processes. Nothing is more foreign to such an analysis than the rejection of causality. But what is important is that these analyses are not about bringing a set of derived phenomena back to one cause but instead about rendering a singular positivity intelligible in precisely what makes it singular.

Let's say roughly that, in opposition to a *genesis* that is oriented toward a unitary primary cause laden with multiple descendants,* it is a question of a *genealogy*—that is, something that tries to restore the conditions of the appearance of a singularity from multiple determining elements from which it emerges not as the product but as the effect.[32] So it's about making things intelligible, but we must see to it that this does not function according to a principle of closure. Closure is not operating here for a certain number of reasons.

The first is that the relations that make it possible to account for this singular effect are, if not in their totality, at least to a considerable extent, relations of interaction between individuals or groups: they entail subjects, types of behavior, decisions, and choices. This network of intelligible relations is not based on or supported by the natural order of things. Rather, its basis is the inherent logic of an interplay of interactions with their constantly changing margins of uncertainty.

There is no closure either, as the the network of relations we are trying to establish to account for a singularity as an effect

* Emphasis in manuscript.

should not just exist on a single plane. These relations are perpetually out of step with each other. The logic of interactions at any given level (say between two individuals) can maintain its rules, specificity, and singular effects at the same time as it interacts with elements occurring at another level. So, in a certain way, because of this, none of these interactions appear as either primary or absolutely totalizing. Each can be resituated in an interplay that goes beyond them. Conversely no interaction, no matter how local, is without effect or without the risk of an effect on the interactions which it participates in and which surround it. So if you like, broadly, we have perpetual mobility, essential fragility, or rather entanglement between what extends a process and what transforms this same process. In short, it's about establishing a form of analyses that could be described as *strategic*.[33]

Speaking of archaeology, strategy, and genealogy, I don't think we need to identify these as three successive levels that develop from each other. Instead we can characterize these as three dimensions of the same analysis that are necessarily simultaneous. In their simultaneity, these dimensions allow us to capture positivities—namely, the conditions that make a singularity acceptable and whose intelligibility is established by identifying the interactions and strategies it's integrated into. We can name the kind of research that takes these three dimensions into account a process of eventalization. [...]* is produced as an effect, and finally eventalization where we are dealing with something whose stability, deep rootedness, and foundation is never such that we cannot, one way or another, if not conceive of its disappearance, at least identify by what

* There is a gap in the recording when the tape was changed to the other side. Only a part of this could be reconstructed from the manuscript.

and under what circumstances its disappearance might be possible.

I said earlier that rather than posing the problem in terms of knowledge [*connaissance*] and legitimation, the question needed to be addressed from the perspective of power and eventalization. But you see it's not about understanding the workings of power as domination, control, a fundamental given, a single principle, an explanation, or an inescapable law. Rather, it always needs to be considered as a relation in a field of interactions existing in an inseperable relation to forms of knowledge [*savoir*]. It must always be conceived in such a way as to be seen to be associated with a field of possibility and as such subject to reversability and possible reversal.[34]

You can see the question is thus no longer: By what error, illusion, oversight, by what failings of legitimacy does knowledge come to give rise to the effects of domination manifested in the modern world by the ascendency of techne? The question is instead: how do knowledge [*savoir*] and power, in the inseparable interplay of their interactions and multiple strategies, give rise to both singularities and a field of possibility? Singularities that are fixed by the conditions that make them acceptable; and a field of possiblities, openings, indecisions, reversals, and possible dislocations rendering them fragile and impermanent, turning these effects into events—nothing more, nothing less than events. How can the effects of coercion inherent in these positivities be inverted or undone within a concrete strategic field, in the concrete strategic field that gave rise to them, starting from the decision not to be governed? How can we avoid seeing these effects dissipated in a return to the legitimate destination of a field of knowledge [*connaissance*] and to a reflection on the transcendental or the quasi-transcendental that fixes this destination?

In conclusion, we note the movement that tipped the crit-

ical attitude into the question of critique, or again the movement that gathered the enterprise of the Aufklärung into the
critical project, which was all about ensuring that knowledge
had the right idea of itself. Shouldn't we now be trying to take
a path in the opposite direction to this tipping over, this shift
and way of carrying the question of Aufklärung off course
into critique? Couldn't we try to go down this route but in the
other direction? And if we need to raise the question of the
relation of knowledge [connaissance] to domination, it would
originate first and foremost from a certain decisive will not to
be governed, this decisive will, which is both individual and
collective, to exit, as Kant said, from minority. It's a question
of attitude. You can now see why I couldn't give, didn't dare
give, my talk a title, a title which would have been: "What Is
Aufklärung?"

HENRI GOUHIER: I would like to thank Michel Foucault
very much for bringing us such a well coordinated set of reflections, reflections that I would personally describe as philosophical, even if he said he wasn't a philosopher. I have to say
right away that after this he added "barely a critic," in short a
bit of a critic after all. And after his presentation I am wondering if being a bit of a critic doesn't actually mean being very
much of a philosopher.*

NOËL MOULOUD: I would like to make maybe two or three
remarks. The first is that M. Foucault seems to have presented
us with a general attitude of thought, a contestation of power
or the contestation of a constraining rule leading to a general
attitude—namely, the critical attitude. He has gone from
there to a problematic that he has presented as an extension of

---

*Discussion reproduced with the kind permission of the Société
française de Philosophie.

this attitude—namely, an updating of this attitude. These are problems that are being raised currently with respect to the relations of knowledge, technology, and power. To a certain extent, I would see localized critical attitudes revolving around certain core problems with largely historical sources or limits if you like. We must already have a practice, a method reaching certain limits and raising problems that lead to dead ends, for a critical attitude to emerge. So, for example, the methodological successes of positivism and the difficulties it has raised has led to the critical reactions that we know. These critical reactions have been around for half a century and include logicist and criticist reflection. I am thinking of the Popperian school or Wittgensteinian reflection on the limits of a normalized scientific language. Often in these critical moments, we see a new resolution appearing: the search for a renewed practice, for a method which itself has a regional aspect, an aspect of historical research.

MICHEL FOUCAULT: You are absolutely right. The critical attitude was certainly engaged on this route, developing its consequences in an exceptional way in the nineteenth century. This is the Kantian channel I'd say: meaning that the high point, the essential moment of the critical attitude needs to be the problem of the interrogation by knowledge [*connaissance*] of its own limits or impasses, if you like, encountered in its primary and concrete exercise.

Two things have struck me. On the one hand, this Kantian usage of the critical attitude did not prevent—and indeed in Kant the problem is very explicitly posed—critique from raising a particular question. (The problem of whether it is fundamental or not can be argued). This question is: How can reason be used? What use of reason can have effects in relation to the abuse of the exercise of power and as a consequence on the concrete destination of freedom? I think Kant was far from being unaware of this problem and that there was, especially in Germany, a whole movement of reflection around this theme, generalizing and shifting the strict critical problem you cited to other areas. You cite Popper, but after all the excess of power was quite a fundamental problem for Popper too.

On the other hand, what I wanted to point out, and I apologize for this being very much of an overview, is that I think we need to look for the historical origins of the critical attitude specifically in its form in the West—and in the modern West since the fifteenth to sixteenth centuries—in the religious struggles and spiritual attitudes of the second half of the Middle Ages. It was at this precise moment that the problem arose of how we are to be governed and whether we agree to be governed in this way. It is then that things were at their most concrete and the most historically determined. All the struggles around the pastoral in the second half of the Middle Ages prepared the way for the Reformation and, I think, were the historical threshold from which this critical attitude developed.[35]

HENRI BIRAULT: I don't want to take on the role of the frightened guinea fowl here! I completely agree about the way the question of the Aufklärung was explicitly taken up by Kant, simultaneously undergoing a decisive theoretical restriction in line with the moral, religious, political, and other imperatives that characterize Kantian thought. I think that we are both in total agreement on this.

Turning now to the most directly substantive part of the presentation that studied the crossfire between knowledge and power at ground level, or at the level of the event. Let's put this in a more essentially or traditionally philosophical way: I wonder if there could still be room for an underlying question that might operate behind the scenes of this valuable and meticulous study of the interplay of knowledge and power in different domains. This metaphysical and historical question could be formulated as follows: Could one say that at a certain moment in our history, and in a certain region of the world, knowledge [*savoir*] in itself, knowledge as such, took on the form of a power [*pouvoir*] or a force [*puissance*]? And then power, for its part still defined as know-how [*savoir-faire*], a certain way of knowing how to go about things and take them on, finally manifested the inherently dynamic essence of the noetic? If this is the case, then it's not surprising Michel Foucault can find and unravel the networks or multiple relationships between knowledge and power, since from a certain period of history at least, knowledge is basically a form of power and power is basically a form of knowledge. Knowledge and power come from the same will, that I am compelled to call the will to power [*puissance*].

MICHEL FOUCAULT: Is your question related to the generality of this type of relation?

HENRI BIRAULT: Not so much its generality as its radicality or its existence as a hidden foundation beneath the duality of the two terms knowledge-power [*savoir-pouvoir*]. Is it possible to find a sort of essence common to knowledge and power, knowledge being defined in itself as knowledge of power and power for its part defining itself as knowledge of power (even if it means carefully exploring the multiple meanings of this double genitive)?

MICHEL FOUCAULT: Absolutely. I was insufficiently clear here, inasmuch as what I wanted to do, what I was suggesting, was that below or beyond a kind of description—basically there are intellectuals and men of power, there are men of science and the demands of industry, and so on. In fact, we have a whole intertwined network, not just elements of knowledge and power. But for knowledge to function as knowledge, it can only do so insofar as it exercises power. Within other discourses of knowledge which exist in relation to possible discourses of knowledge, each statement [*énoncé*] considered to be true exercises a certain power at the same time as it creates a possibility. Conversely, any exercise of power, even if it is a killing, involves at least one skill [*savoir-faire*]: after all, savagely crushing an individual still requires a certain way of knowing how to go about it. So, if you like, I totally agree and that's what I was trying to show. Beneath polarities that seem to me to be quite distinct from the polarities of power, there's a kind of shimmer . . .

NOËL MOULOUD: I want to come back to the reference M. Birault and I both have in common: Popper. One of Popper's intentions is to show that in establishing spheres of power, whatever their nature, whether dogmas, imperative norms, paradigms, it's not knowledge [*savoir*] itself that's active and responsible but a deviant rationality which is no longer truly knowledge. Knowledge—or rationality as formative—is itself devoid of paradigms and devoid of recipes. Its inherent approach is to question its own convictions and authority and to "argue against itself." It is precisely for this reason that it is rationality: methodology such as Popper conceives of it decides between and separates these two behaviors, making it impossible to confuse and mix the use of recipes, the management of procedures, and the invention of reasons. And I wonder, if the social sciences as a whole don't equally and primarily play the role of opening things up in the human, social, and historical field, even if this is much more difficult. It's a very difficult situation because sciences and technology are in fact interdependent. The relationship between a science and the powers that use it is not really essential. Even if it is important, in a certain way it remains "contingent." Instead it's the technical conditions of knowledge use that directly relate to the exercise of power, a power eluding exchange or examination, rather than the conditions of knowledge itself, and it's in this sense that I don't quite understand the argument. But M. Foucault made some enlightening remarks that he will undoubtedly go on to develop. But I am wondering: Is there really a direct link between the obligations and claims of knowledge and those of power?

MICHEL FOUCAULT: I would be delighted if we could do things like this, if we could say, "There is good science, one that is both true and has nothing to do with nasty power; and then, of course, the bad uses of science, either in terms of self-interested applications or errors." If you can tell me that's how it is, well, I'll go home happy.

NOËL MOULOUD: No I wasn't saying that. I recognize that the historical link, the event driven link is strong. But I have noticed several things: that new scientific investigations (in biology and the human sciences) are once again placing man and society in a situation of nondetermination, opening paths of freedom, thus constraining them, as it were, to make decisions again. Besides, oppressive powers rarely rely on scientific knowledge but prefer to rely on a lack of knowledge, on a science that has been reduced to a "myth" beforehand. We are all familiar with the examples of racism based on "pseudogenetics" or political pragmatism based on a "neo-Lamarckian" deformation of biology and so on. Finally, I am well aware that the concrete knowledge of science calls for the distance of critical judgment. But it seems to me—and this was the gist of my argument—that a humanist critique, which rests on cultural and axiological criteria, cannot develop fully or succeed without the support provided by knowledge itself in undertaking the critique of its bases, its presuppositions and its antecedents. This especially concerns the clarifications the human sciences and history bring to the table; and I think Habermas in particular, includes this analytical dimension in what he describes as the critique of ideologies, even those generated by knowledge.

MICHEL FOUCAULT: I think that's precisely the advantage of critique!

HENRI GOUHIER: I would like to ask you a question. I totally agree with the distinctions you have made and the importance of the Reformation. But it seems to me that there's been a critical fermentation throughout the whole Western tradition—one brought about by Socratism. I wanted to ask you if the word "critique," as you have defined and used it, might not be suitable for what I would provisionally describe as a critical fermentation by Socratism in all of Western thought? This would then go on to play a role in the return to Socrates in the sixteenth to seventeenth centuries.

MICHEL FOUCAULT: You've got me with a more difficult question. I'd say that this return of Socratism (it seems to me you can historically sense, see, and identify it at the turn of the sixteenth to seventeeth centuries) was only possible on the basis of something that was much more important in my opinion, and that was the pastoral struggles and the problem of government, in the very fullest and largest sense this term took on in the late Middle Ages. To govern people was to take them by the hand, to lead them to their salvation through an operation, a detailed technique of guidance, which involved a whole mechanics [jeu] of knowledge—in relation to the individual being guided and to the truth they were being guided toward . . .

HENRI GOUHIER: Could you reapply your analysis to a presentation on Socrates and his times?

MICHEL FOUCAULT: This is indeed the real problem. Here again, to respond quickly on this difficult matter, I think basically that when we examine Socrates like this, or even—I hardly dare say it—and I wonder if Heidegger examining the Presocratics doesn't . . . no, I don't think so, we should avoid the anachronism of projecting the eighteenth century into the fifth . . . But I wonder if this question of the Aufklärung that has, I think, been quite fundamental to Western philosophy since Kant, I wonder if it hasn't been used to somehow gather up all possible history right back to the primordial origins of philosophy. So you could, I think, validly examine Socrates's trial without anachronism, but on the basis of a problem which is, and which was in any case perceived by Kant, as being a problem related to the Aufklärung.[36]

JEAN-LOUIS BRUCH: I would like to ask you a question about a formulation that was central to your presentation, but which was expressed in two ways that seemed different to me. At the end you spoke about "the decisive will not to be governed" as a foundation, or a reversal of the Aufklärung which was the subject of your talk. At the beginning you spoke of "not being governed like this," "not being governed quite so much," "not being governed at this price." In one case, the formulation is absolute, in the other it is relative, but according to what criteria? Have you arrived at this radical position, the decisive will not to be governed because of the experience of the abuse of governmentization? I'm wondering about this. And finally, shouldn't this latter position itself be the subject of an examination and be called into question which itself would be an essentially philosophical move?

MICHEL FOUCAULT: These are two good questions. In response to your point on the variations in my formulation: I don't think, in fact, that the will not to be governed at all is something that can be regarded as an innate aspiration. I think in fact the desire not to be governed is always the will not to be governed like this, by them, at this price. As for the formulation of not being governed at all, in a way this seems to me to be the philosophical and theoretical pinnacle of something like the will not to be relatively governed. When I said at the end "the decisive will not to be governed," this was an error on my part, it should have been "not to be governed thus, like this, in this way." I was not referring to something like a fundamental anarchism, or an originary freedom that was absolutely and fundamentally resistant to any governmentalization. I didn't say this, but that doesn't mean I am absolutely excluding it. I think my presentation ended there, because it had already gone on for too long; but also because I wonder . . . If we wanted to explore this dimension of critique I believe to be so important both because it's part of philosophy and also not part of it. In emploring this dimension of critique and the base of the critical attitude, we might be referred back to something like the historical practice of revolt and the nonacceptance of a real government, on the one hand, and on the other, the individual experience of the rejection of governmentality. What really strikes me—but I may be obsessed because these are things I am deeply preoccupied with at present—is the fact that if the matrix of the critical attitude in the Western world is to be sought in the Middle Ages in religious attitudes and in connection with the exercise of pastoral power, it's still very surprising to see the individual and political experience of mysticism and institutional struggle operating as one. They were both absolutely integral to each other, or at any rate perpetually referring to each other. I would say that one of the first great forms of revolt in the West was mysticism.[37] All these hotbeds of resistance to the authority of scripture and mediation by the pastor were developed either in convents and monasteries or outside these institutions among the laity. I think there is something quite fundamental in all of these experiences and spiritual movements that provide the trappings and vocabulary, and even more, the ways of being and mediums of hope for what could be described as economic and popular struggles, or to put it in Marxist terms, "class" struggles.

In the trajectory of this critical attitude whose history starts at this time I think, perhaps we should now be examining what the will not to be governed like this and so on might be both in its individual and collective forms of experience. We must now raise the problem of the will.[38] In short, and you might say this was self-evident, we can't revisit this problem in the context of power without of course, raising the question of the will. This is so obvious that I should have picked up on it before. But since this problem of will is a problem that Western philosophy has always treated with infinite precautions and difficulty, let's just say that I've tried to avoid it as much as possible. Let's just say [this question] is inevitable. I have given you a few considerations here on work in progress.

ANDRÉ SERNIN: What side would you rather be on? Would you be on Auguste Comte's side, and I'm generalizing here, rigorously separating spiritual power from temporal power; or on Plato's side, who said things would never be right until philosophers themselves were in power as temporal leaders?

MICHEL FOUCAULT: Do I really have to choose?

ANDRÉ SERNIN: No, you don't, but which side would you be more inclined to take?

MICHEL FOUCAULT: I'd try to dodge my way between them!

PIERRE HADJI-DIMOU: You have successfully presented us

with the problem of critique and its links to philosophy, and you have ended up with the relationships between power and knowledge [connaissance]. I wanted to shed a little light on Greek thought. I think this problem has already been raised by our chairman [Henri Gouhier]. "To know" [connaître] is to be in possession of logos and mythos. I think that with the Aufklärung, we don't end up knowing. Knowledge isn't just rationality, it's not just the logos in historical life, there's a second source, the mythos. If we refer to the discussion between Protagoras and Socrates, when Protagoras asks the question about the politeia's right to punish and its power, he says that he is going to clarify and illustrate his thinking in relation to mythos.[39] Mythos is linked to logos because there is a rationality: the more it teaches us, the more wonderful it is. Here is the question I wanted to add: In suppressing a part of thought, the irrational thinking that arrives at logos, that is, mythos, do we get to know the sources of knowledge, the knowledge of power that also has a mythical meaning itself?

MICHEL FOUCAULT: I agree with your question.

SYLVAIN ZAC: I would like to make two comments. You have quite rightly observed that critical thinking can be considered as a virtue. Now there is a philosopher, Malebranche, who studied this virtue: it is the freedom of mind. In addition, I don't agree with you on the relationships you have established between Kant's article on the Enlightenment and his critique of knowledge [connaissance]. The latter obviously sets limits but has no limits itself; it is total. But when you read the article on the Enlightenment, you can see that Kant makes a very important distinction between public use and private use. In the case of public use, this courage needs to vanish. Which means . . .

MICHEL FOUCAULT: It's the opposite, because what he describes as public use is . . .

SYLVAIN ZAC: For example, when someone holds a chair in philosophy at a university, when he exercises the public use of speech he mustn't criticize the Bible; but he can do so in private.

MICHEL FOUCAULT: It's the opposite, and that's what's so interesting. Indeed, Kant says, "There is a public use of reason that should not be limited." What is this public use? It's what circulates between scholars and is disseminated via newspapers and publications appealing to everyone's conscience. These uses, these public uses of reason should not be limited, and curiously what he calls private use is the civil servant's use as it were. The civil servant, the officer, he says, has no right to say to his superior, "I'm not obeying you and your order is absurd." Curiously he defines private use as the obedience of each individual, insofar as he is part of the state, to his superior, the sovereign or the sovereign's representative.[40]

SYLVAIN ZAC: I agree with you, I was wrong, but it still follows that there are still limits to the display of courage in this article. I found these limits everywhere, in all the *Aufklärer*, in Mendelssohn obviously. There is an element of conformity in the German Aufklärung, that one doesn't find even in the eighteenth-century French Enlightenment.

MICHEL FOUCAULT: I totally agree, but I don't really see how it contradicts what I've said.

SYLVAIN ZAC: I don't believe there's a close historical link between the movement of Aufklärung you've placed at the center of the development of the critical attitude and the attitude of resistance from either an intellectual or political point of view. Don't you think that this clarification could be added?

MICHEL FOUCAULT: I don't think that Kant felt that he was a stranger to the Aufklärung. It was part of his contemporary landscape and he was actively participating in it, not only in this article on the Aufklärung, but from many other angles . . .

SYLVAIN ZAC: The word "Aufklärung" is found in *Religion within the Bounds of Bare Reason*,[41] but there it applies to the purity of feelings, to something internal. An inversion has taken place as with Rousseau.

MICHEL FOUCAULT: I would like to finish what I was saying . . . So Kant felt perfectly in tune with the contemporary landscape he described as the Aufklärung and that he was trying to define. I think he introduced a dimension we could consider as more specific or, on the contrary, as more general and more radical in relation to this movement of Aufklärung. So the first bold step that needs to be implemented when it comes to knowledge [*savoir*] and fields of knowledge [*connaissance*], is to know [*connaître*] what one is able to know. That's the radicality and for Kant himself the universality of his enterprise. I believe in this relationship, whatever the limits to the boldness of the *Aufklärer* might have been of course. I don't see how the timidities of the *Aufklärer* could change anything in the kind of move made by Kant and which I believe, he was fairly well aware of.

HENRI BIRAULT: I think in fact that critical philosophy is a movement that both restricts and radicalizes the Aufklärung in general.

MICHEL FOUCAULT: But its link to the Aufklärung was a general question at the time. What are we talking about, what is this movement that came just before us and which we still belong to called the Aufklärung? The best proof is that the newspaper had a series of articles that it was able to publish, Mendelssohn's and Kant's. This was a topical issue.[42] A bit like for us, when we raise the question of the crisis in current values.

JEANNE DUBOUCHET: I would like to ask you what content do you associate with knowledge? Power, as I understood it, was a question of not being governed, but what kind of order of knowledge [*savoir*]?

MICHEL FOUCAULT: As it happens, if I'm using this word, once again it's essentially to neutralize everything that might either legitimize or even simply organize values in a hierarchy. If you like, for me—as scandalous as this may and indeed should appear in the eyes of a scholar, a methodologist or even a historian of science—for me, when I'm talking about knowledge [*savoir*], I'm provisionally avoiding making a distinction between a psychiatrist's proposition and a mathematical demonstration. The only point where I would introduce differences would be to determine the power effects of induction, if you like. This is not induction in the logical sense of the term, or in the sense that this proposition takes on in the scientific domain of its formulation—mathematics, psychiatry, and so on. I would like to determine the institutional, nondiscursive, nonformalizable, not especially scientific networks of institutional power induction is linked to as soon as it is put into circulation. This is what I would describe as knowledge [*savoir*]: the elements of domains of knowledge [*connaissance*] which, whatever their value in relation to us, in relation to a pure mind, exercise effects of power within their domain and beyond.

HENRI GOUHIER: I think it remains to me to thank Michel Foucault for providing us with such an interesting session, which is certain to lead to a publication of particular importance.

MICHEL FOUCAULT: Thank you.

THE CULTURE
OF THE SELF

Lecture by Michel Foucault at the University
of California, Berkeley, on April 12, 1983

In a dialogue written at the end of the second century AD, Lucian presents us with a certain Hermotimus, who is walking down the street mumbling. One of his friends, Lycinus, sees him, crosses the street, and asks, "What are you mumbling about?" And the answer comes, "I am trying to remember what I need to tell my master." From the conversation between Hermotimus and Lycinus, we learn that Hermotimus has been visiting his master for twenty years and has been nearly ruined by the very high cost of those precious lessons. We learn he may need another twenty years to arrive at the end of his training. But we also learn what those lessons are about. Hermotimus is being taught by his master how to take care of himself in the best possible way.[1] I am sure that none of you is a modern Hermotimus, but I can bet most of you have met at least someone who currently regularly visits some kind of master, who takes their money to teach them how to take care of themselves. Fortunately, I have forgotten the words in French, English, and German for these modern masters. In antiquity they were called philosophers.

To explain why I am interested in the theme of the culture of the self as a philosophical and historical question, I'd like to take as a point of departure a short text written by Kant in 1784. The text is "Was ist Aufklärung."[2] This text was an answer to a question published by the *Berlinische Monatsschrift*. Moses Mendelssohn also provided his own answer to this question published two months before Kant's.[3] I think a certain attention needs to be paid to this text. First, it is worth emphasizing that the German philosophical movement through Kant and the Jewish Haskalah through Moses Mendelssohn encountered the same topic at the same time: "Was ist Aufklärung?"[4] It is also worth paying attention to this kind of philosophical interrogation of the present.[5] I know, of course, this is not the first time philosophers have asked questions about their own present, and the historical, religious, or philosophical meaning of the present, but most of the time these interrogations either dealt with comparisons between the present moment and the previous one, or the announcement of a future through signs that needed deciphering. Most of the time, the question of the present was a question about decline or improvement, the proximity of a new age or the arrival of the promised last days. In Kant's text, the question is put in terms of a very specific achievement in the general history of reason, or more precisely in the general history of the way we use our reason. This kind of interrogation is interesting on two grounds. First, the eighteenth century is very often credited with the universal conception of reason, and this assumption is correct. But the eighteenth century was also aware of the historical changes in the use of reason, and Kant's representation of those historical changes is very different from a simple progress or development of reason. I think that there is another justification for paying attention to Kant's text on Enlightenment. This text, I think, introduced a new kind of question into the field of philosophical reflection: the question of the nature, meaning, and

historical and philosophical significance of the precise moment when the philosopher is writing and of which he himself is a part. I don't mean that earlier philosophers were not
aware of their own present and that they didn't worry about
it. Hobbes, Descartes, Spinoza, and Leibniz all took their own
situation and that of the contemporary world into account, as
did Plato and Augustine. For Descartes the failure of several
so-called sciences, for Hobbes the political situation in En-
gland, and for Leibniz religious debates and quarrels were reasons for them to intervene and to try and change the situation.

I think Kant's question in relation to the Aufklärung meant
something else. At the same time, Kant provided a justification for his own philosophical task by analyzing the contemporary reality [actualité] to which he belonged.⁶ His aim in his
philosophical work was to play a certain role in the natural and
spontaneous history of reason. In his short paper on the Enlightenment, Kant raised a set of questions which are, I think,
characteristic of modern philosophy. Those questions were:
What is our present reality [actualité] as a historical figure?
What are we and what do we have to be as part of this present
reality? Why is it necessary to philosophize and what is the
specific task of philosophy in relation to this present reality?
These questions, I think, didn't simply remain embedded and
buried in this rather obscure text, but took on more and more
importance in Western philosophy. When Fichte analyzed the
French Revolution,⁷ it wasn't just because he was concerned
by this rather extraordinary event, it wasn't only that he felt he
had to choose between being either a supporter or an enemy
of the French Revolution, but he also needed to know who
he was himself and what the role of his own philosophy was
in relation to this event. In a certain way, Hegel's philosophy
was an attempt to answer the very simple question: What

was the meaning of the day Napoleon entered Jena after his victory? The *Weltgeist* riding a horse.[8] It was also, I think, Auguste Comte's question, it was Nietzsche's and Max Weber's question, it was also Husserl's question, at least in *The Crisis*. This question has been one of the main trends in Western philosophy from Fichte down to Husserl. I don't mean that these questions became philosophy itself, but they have been a permanent aspect of philosophical activity for the last two centuries. I would suggest there has been a split in Western philosophy since Kant, not so much as a result of the *Critique* itself but as a result of this historico-critical question: What are we now? From the beginning of the nineteenth century, I think, we find two related poles in the field of philosophical activity that cannot be reduced to each other. At one pole you find questions such as: What is truth? How is it possible to know the truth? This pole sees philosophy as a formal ontology of truth or as a critical analysis of knowledge. At the other pole, you find questions such as: What is our present reality [*actualité*]? What are we as part of this present reality? What is the aim of our activity of philosophizing insofar as we are part of our present reality? These questions deal with what I would call the historical ontology of ourselves or the critical history of thought.[9]

I have undertaken several historical inquiries into madness, medicine, crime and punishment, and sexuality within the framework of this second type of question. Of course, there have been—and still are—several ways of elaborating these questions about our historical ontology. But I think that any ontological history of ourselves must analyze three sets of relations: our relations to truth, our relations to obligation, our relations to ourselves and to others.[10] Or, to put it another way, in order to answer the question, What are we now? we need to consider the fact that we are thinking beings, since it is through thought that we look for truth, accept or reject obligations, laws, coercions, and relate to ourselves and others. My aim is not to answer the general question, What is a thinking being? My aim is to answer the question, How did the history of our thought—I mean of our relation to truth, obligations, ourselves and others—make us what we are? In brief: How can we analyze the formation of ourselves through the history of our thought? By "thought," I don't mean exclusively philosophy, theoretical thinking, or scientific knowledge. I don't want to analyze what people think as opposed to what they do, but what they think when they do what they are doing.[11] What I want to analyze is the meaning they attach to their own behavior, the way they integrate their behavior into general strategies, the type of rationality they recognize in their different practices, institutions, models, and behavior.* When I was studying madness and psychiatry, crime and punishment, I was led to emphasize the analysis of our relation first to truth and then to obligation. Studying the constitution of our experience of sexuality now, I am more and more inclined to pay attention to the relation to oneself and the techniques which have shaped those relations.[12]

To analyze these techniques of the self, I'd like to start by choosing a notion that was very important in Greek and Roman culture. I'll try to give you a very brief sketch of the problems linked to this notion, and then maybe we could elaborate on this initial summary in the meetings and seminars over the next few weeks.[13] The notion I have chosen to

---

* Manuscript: My problem is to analyze the types of conduct, the relation to the truth, law, and obligation and to ourselves across social practices, institutions.

begin with is what the Greeks called *epimeleia heautou* and the Latins, *cura sui*.[14] It is not very easy to translate these terms, but I'll try: *epimeleia heautou* means something like "the concern with oneself," or, as we say in French, *le souci de soi*. The verb form *epimeleisthai heautou* means something like "to be concerned with oneself," "to take care of oneself," "*s'occuper de soi-même*." The precept that one must take care of oneself and be concerned with oneself, the precept that one has to *epimeleisthai heautou*, was one of the main principles of ethics for the Greeks and Romans and one of the main rules for their art of life for almost a thousand years.

Let's have a look at some indicative points in this very long period. First, Socrates himself. In the *Apology* written by Plato, we see Socrates presenting himself to his judges as the master of the concern with oneself. He addresses passers-by telling them, "You concern yourselves with your riches, reputation and honors, but you do not concern yourself with your virtue or your soul." Socrates watches over his fellow citizens to make sure that they take care of themselves. He considers that it is *this* task that has been conferred on him by the god and he will not abandon it until his last breath.[15]

Eight centuries later, the same notion of concern with oneself, *epimeleia heautou*, occupies an equally important role in the work of a Christian author, Gregory of Nyssa. But here it has a very different meaning. By this term, Gregory of Nyssa means the movement through which one renounces marriage, detaches oneself from the flesh, and through which, thanks to a virginity of heart and body, one recovers the immortality one has been deprived of.[16] In another passage from the same treatise, *On Virginity*, Gregory uses the parable of the lost drachma as the model for the concern with oneself. To find a lost drachma, you must light a lamp, turn the whole house upside down, search in every corner until gleaming in the shadows you see the metal of the coin. In the same way, to recover the effigy which God has printed on our soul, and which the body has tarnished, one must take care of oneself, light the lamp of reason, and search every corner of the soul.[17]

Between these two extreme points of reference, Socrates and Gregory of Nyssa, you can see that the concern with oneself was not just a constant principle but a widespread practice. The principle of occupying oneself with oneself was almost universally accepted by those philosophers who claimed to be advisers on life and guides to existence. Following their master, the Epicureans repeated that it was never too early and never too late to occupy oneself with one's own soul. Musonius Rufus, a Stoic, also says: "it is in constantly paying attention to oneself that one assures one's salvation."[18] Or Seneca: "You must attend to your soul, attend to yourself, lose no time in doing so, retire into yourself and stay there."[19] Dio of Prusa devotes a lecture to the necessity of an *anakhōrēsis eis heauton*, a retreat into oneself.[20] Galen, calculating how much time is necessary to train a doctor, orator, or grammarian, thinks that even more time is necessary to become a good man: "Years and years," he says, "spent in occupying yourself with yourself."[21] Epictetus, in one of his *Diatribai*, offers this definition of the human being: "Man is this unique being on earth who needs to take care of himself."[22] Nature has provided animals with everything they need, humans don't have the same natural equipment, but we must understand the necessity of taking care of ourselves has also been bestowed as a supplementary gift. God has confided us to ourselves, by this means giving us the possibility and the duty of being free. For Epictetus, the *epimeleia heautou*, which is ontologically linked to human finitude, is the practical form of freedom, and it is by taking

care of himself that the human being becomes like God—
a god who has nothing other to do than take care of himself.
For us now, the notion of *epimeleia heautou* has faded and
become obscure. It seems to have been effaced by both the
Socratic precept of *gnōthi seauton* and by the Christian principles of asceticism which imply renouncing oneself. If we are
asked "What was the most important moral principle that was
most characteristic of ancient philosophy?" the answer that
comes immediately to mind is not *epimelē seautō*, "take care of
yourself," but, as you know, *gnōthi seauton*, know yourself. Perhaps our philosophical and historical tradition has overrated
the importance of the *gnōthi seauton*, of "know yourself." One
needs to remember that in ancient culture the rule of having
to know oneself was in fact, constantly associated with that of
concerning oneself with oneself, and more than that, knowing
oneself was considered as a means of taking care of oneself.[23]
When we consider Christian asceticism, we are accustomed
to emphasizing the rule of renouncing oneself and forget that
in the spiritual experience of some early Christians like Gregory of Nyssa, renouncing oneself was a way of taking care of
oneself, or at least a new form of the old philosophical *epimeleia heautou*. I think we have to be aware that those two great
figures of the Western experience of the self, self-knowledge
and asceticism, are rooted in this multisecular tradition of the
care of the self. In Greco-Roman culture, the care of the self
is at the same time a notion, a precept, an attitude, and a technique—a practical matrix for the experience of the self. Most
historians of ancient philosophy are concerned with the rise
of ontology and metaphysics from Parmenides to Aristotle
through Plato. Most historians of the Greek sciences are interested in the rise of rational thought through mathematics
and cosmology. I think it might also be valuable to study the

rise of a certain type of subjectivity, of a certain type of relation to the self, in this Greco-Latin culture of the self. Greek metaphysics has determined our philosophical relationship to being, Greek science has determined our rational relationship to the world. The Greco-Roman culture of the self has, I think, determined our ethical relationship to ourselves. If I could find people interested in the same topics, my dream would be to start a historical analysis of these techniques of the self[24] in Western societies from the beginning of Greek civilization.[25]

My intention tonight is to present you with a very brief survey of some aspects of this culture of the self in Greek and Greco-Roman civilization. I'll take just two aspects of this culture of the self, one in the fourth century BC and the other in the first two centuries AD.

It has been sometimes claimed that the culture of the self in Greco-Roman society was linked to the decay of the old political and social structures. The decline of the cities and the old traditional aristocracies, the development of autocratic regimes and the increasing importance of private life—all of these could have been factors in the rise of a so-called individualism. But my hypothesis is that these historical processes, if they really took place, may indeed have produced some changes in the culture of the self, but they are not in themselves the reason for the high value attributed to the care of the self.[26] The care of the self was very well known and very highly valued from at least the fourth century BC. For instance, according to Plutarch, when a Spartan king was asked why Spartans didn't cultivate their land themselves but let the Helots do the job for them, he answered, "The reason we do not cultivate our land is that we prefer to take care of ourselves."[27] In Xenophon's *Cyropaedia*, we see Cyrus (the model of a great king, and a good man, according to Xenophon) coming back to his palace after several great victories and conquests, meeting old friends and companions and asking them, "Well, what shall we do now?" Cyrus himself gives the answer. The answer is not, "Well, I'll take care, or we'll take care of the new empire." He says, "And now that we have been victorious, we must take care of ourselves."[28] The culture of the self was not a late phenomenon in the wake of the decline of the classical city; it was an early phenomenon taking several forms in antiquity.

The first philosophical elaboration of the principle "you must concern yourself with yourself" is to be found in a dialogue written by Plato, in the *Alcibiades*.[29] The Neoplatonists considered this dialogue to be the first in Plato's works. Albinus, a second century Neoplatonist said "every naturally gifted young man" who had reached the age of philosophizing and practicing virtue should begin by studying the *Alcibiades*. Proclus considered this dialogue to be the *archē apasēs philosophias*—meaning the principle and point of departure for all philosophy—as this dialogue teaches people to be concerned with themselves.[30] In fact, and in spite of the late subtitle given to this text, *Peri anthropinēs phuseōs*, on human nature, the theme and topic of the entire dialogue is the *epimeleia heautou*. Socrates tries to convince Alcibiades that he must take care of himself. I would like to draw attention to only three or four points in this analysis of the *epimeleia heautou*.

The first is this: Why should Alcibiades take care of himself? The reason given by Socrates is that he is at a point of transition in his life. Alcibiades is not satisfied with the privileges afforded him by his birth, fortune, and status. He says specifically that he does not want to spend his life, *katabiōnai*, profiting from all this. Alcibiades wishes to gain the advantage over all others inside the city and out, including the kings of Sparta and the Persian sovereign. But Alcibiades very soon demonstrated he was unable to succeed in this attempt. He hadn't received the good education young Spartans enjoyed. He had been entrusted to a completely ignorant old slave and didn't even know what the words "justice" and "concord" meant. Discovering how ignorant he was, Alcibiades was greatly embarrassed. He despaired, but Socrates intervened and gives him this important advice: "If you were fifty years old, the situation would be serious. Then it would be too late. But you are still very young, and this is precisely the moment when you have to *epimeleisthai heautou*, take care of yourself." So, as you can see, the obligation of caring for oneself is directly linked to the young man's age, his project of ruling the city, and to a defective pedagogy.

But how could Alcibiades take care of himself? Nobody was ready to help him, at least among the crowd of followers he had while he was still very young. When the dialogue starts, Alcibiades is around sixteen or seventeen, he has grown up, he has beard on his cheeks, he is not desirable anymore. That is precisely the reason why Socrates intervenes: Socrates has a philosophical love for Alcibiades and is able to help him in taking care of himself. So, as you see, the care of the self is directly linked to a kind of personal relation, the master's personal and philosophical love of the disciple. But Socrates and Alcibiades need to make clear precisely what the "concern for oneself" is and what this "concern for oneself" consists of. Socrates explains the self is nothing other than a soul, and taking care of the soul implies that one can discover what this soul really is. Therefore, one must contemplate one's own soul or, better, the divine element which is the reality of the soul.

In brief, we can see that in the *Alcibiades* the care of the self is clearly linked to the political ambition of a young aristocrat: If you want to rule others, you need to first take care of yourself. Second, the concern with the self is linked to a defective pedagogy: you must take care of yourself as your education has been unable to teach you what you need to know. Third, it is linked to an erotic and philosophical relation between the youth and teacher and takes the principal form of the soul's self-contemplation.

The culture of the self that appears in the Greco-Roman culture of the first two centuries AD is, I think, profoundly different from what we have encountered with Alcibiades, Socrates, and Plato. In comparison with the Socratic *epimeleia tēs psuchēs*, the culture of the self practiced by Seneca, Dio of Prusa, Epictetus, Plutarch, Marcus Aurelius, Galen, and others seems to be different on the very points I have just mentioned. Thus, it can be considered an important step toward what will come to be seen as the Christian technology of the self. The new, or partially new, culture of the self we observe in Greco-Roman culture in the first two centuries AD implies, first, a permanent relationship to oneself, and not just a preparation to become a good ruler of the city. Second, it implies a critical relationship to the self, not just a complement to a defective pedagogy. Third, it implies a relationship of authority with the master (not an erotic relation). And fourth, it implies a set of ascetic practices that are very different from pure contemplation of the soul. I think these four ideas of a permanent relationship to the self, a critical relationship to the self, a relationship of authority with another in order to take care of oneself, and this idea that the care of the self is not just pure contemplation but a set of practices, all of this is characteristic not only of the culture of the self in the first centuries AD but also of the Christian care of the self and, in a certain way, of our own culture of the self.[31]

First point, the care of the self must be a permanent relationship to oneself. Socrates, you would remember, recom-

mended to Alcibiades that he profit from his youth and occupy himself with himself. At fifty, it would be too late. But
Epicurus, on the contrary—writing not long after Socrates,
in the third century BC—says, "When you are young, you
must not hesitate to philosophize, and when you are old, you
must not hesitate to philosophize. It is never too early or too
late to concern yourself with your soul."[32] It is this principle
of perpetual attention to oneself throughout one's life which
very clearly gains the upper hand. For example, Musonius
Rufus says, "You must take care of yourself without ceasing
if you are to lead a life conducive to well-being."[33] And Galen,
"In order to become an accomplished man, every man must,
as it were, exert himself his whole life."[34] This is the case,
even if it is true that it would been much better to have kept
watch over one's soul from an early age. In fact, the friends
to whom Seneca or Plutarch gave advice were no longer the
ambitious and desirable young men addressed by Socrates.[35]
They were men, sometimes young (like Serenus), sometimes
fully mature (like Lucilius, who held the very important position of procurator in Sicily when he and Seneca engaged in
a long spiritual correspondence). Epictetus kept a school for
young people, that's true, but sometimes he had occasion to
address adults and even consular figures reminding them of
their task of occupying themselves with themselves. Marcus
Aurelius brought together his notes—and in so doing he was
exercising the function of emperor and for him it was a question of coming to his own aid. Being occupied with oneself is
not therefore a simple and momentary preparation for life; it
is a form of life. Alcibiades realized that he ought to occupy
himself with himself insofar as he wanted consequently to occupy himself with others. It becomes a question of occupying
yourself *with* yourself and *for* yourself.

From this, comes the very important idea of changing one's

attitude toward oneself, *ad se convertere*, the idea of a movement in one's existence where one returns to oneself as the ultimate goal. You will tell me that the *epistrophē*, this conversion, is a typically Platonic theme. But, as we have seen in the *Alcibiades*, the movement through which the soul turns toward itself is also a movement that attracts its gaze toward light, reality, the divine element, essence, and the supercelestial world where essences are visible. The turning back that Seneca, Plutarch, and Epictetus invite is quite different.[36] It is a kind of turning round on the spot. It has no end or conclusion other than taking up residence in oneself and staying there. The final objective of conversion to oneself is to establish a certain number of relations to oneself. Sometimes these relations are conceived of according to a juridico-political model: the aim is to become sovereign over oneself and exercise complete mastery over oneself, to be fully independent and completely one's own (*fieri suum*, as Seneca often says). They are also often represented following the model of the enjoyment of possessions: to enjoy oneself, take pleasure in oneself, and find the satisfaction of one's desire in oneself. In this form of thought, in this form of culture of the self, the relation to oneself is oriented toward a kind of internal finality.

A second big difference is related to pedagogy. In the *Alcibiades*, the concern with oneself was necessary because of faulty pedagogy, complementing teaching and acting as a substitute, in any case, offering a form of training. From the moment the concern with the self becomes an adult practice to be undertaken one's whole life, its pedagogical role tends to be effaced and other functions appear.

First, a critical function. The culture of the self should allow one not only to acquire new knowledge, but better, to get rid of all bad habits and false opinions derived from the crowd, from bad masters, and from one's relatives and entourage. To unlearn, *dediscere*, is one of the important tasks in the development of oneself.

But [the culture of the self] also has the function of a struggle. The practice of oneself is now conceived of as a permanent fight. It is not simply a question of training a man of value for the future. The individual must be provided with the weapons and courage that will enable him to fight his entire life. You are aware, no doubt, of the frequency of two metaphors: the athletic contest—in life one is like a wrestler who must free himself from successive adversaries and keep in training even when not in combat. The second is the metaphor of war—the self must be organized like an army, which may at any moment be assailed by the enemy. Thus, the great Christian theme of the spiritual combat of the soul and the spiritual struggle of the soul, is already a fundamental principle of the culture of the self in ancient pagan times.

Above all, this culture of the self has a curative and therapeutic function.[37] It is much closer to the medical model than the pedagogical one. One must of course remember a few facts about Greek culture that are extremely ancient: namely, the existence of the notion of *pathos*, which signifies the passion of the soul as well as bodily illness. We have the breadth of a metaphorical field allowing expressions such as "cure," "look after," "amputate," "scarify," "purge," and so on to be applied to body and soul. One must also remember the principle familiar to the Epicureans, Cynics, and Stoics that the role of philosophy is to heal the maladies of the soul. Thus, Plutarch was able to say that philosophy and medicine constitute *mia khōra*, a single area, a single field.[38] But I would also like to insist on the practical correlation between medicine and the culture of the self. Epictetus did not want his school to be considered simply as a school or training place. Rather, he wanted his school to be considered as a doctor's consulting room, what he called an *iatreion*, he wanted it to be a dispensary for the soul, and his pupils to be aware of the fact they were ill. One of them, he said, has a shoulder out of joint, the second an abscess, the third a fistula, another a headache. And all of them wish to learn syllogisms. The first cure they need is a medical cure. They have to cure their wounds, they have to stop the flow of their humors, they have to calm their spirits.[39] Conversely, a doctor such as Galen considered it to be within his competence to heal the soul from the passions, from disordered energies, rebels to reason, and also errors born of false opinions. In the treatise *On the Passions and Errors of the Soul*, Galen boasts of cures he has successfully conducted: he cured one of his companions inclined to anger, he healed a young man whose soul was troubled by events of little importance.[40] All these ideas may now appear very familiar, and indeed they are, but I think it's very important in considering the history of subjectivity in the West to pick up the first links between the experience of the self and medical practice. It is important to catch the moment and the conditions that led to the emergence of the links of the relations between medical practice and the inner experience of oneself.

And now I would like to discuss the third point I raised earlier. I would like to rapidly indicate the third great difference between the occupation with oneself in the *Alcibiades* and the practice of the self in the culture of the imperial period. As you remember, in Plato's dialogue, the erotico-philosophical relationship with the master was essential. It established the framework that allowed Socrates and Alcibiades to take charge of the soul of the young man together. In the first and second centuries AD, the relation to the self always relied on the relationship with a master or a director—in any case with someone else—but became more and more independent of the amorous relationship.[41] It was very generally admitted that one could not occupy oneself with oneself without the help of another. Seneca said that nobody was sufficiently strong to free themselves from the state of *stultitia*.[42] But these necessary relationships between the disciple and master are technical, sometimes administrative and institutional relations, and have nothing to do with the erotic relation. There are some strictly scholastic organizations, for instance the school of Epictetus, which serve as an example. In Epictetus's school there was a set of hierarchical relations and different forms of training, there was a visiting audience alongside pupils who were received for longer courses. But teaching was also dispensed to those who wanted to become philosophers and spiritual directors.* Some of the discourses collected by Arrian are technical lessons for future practitioners of the culture of the self. You can also find private counselors in the entourage of a few great figures, mostly in Rome, as part of their group or clientele. As you can see, nothing to do with erotic relations.

And the last point. We must not imagine that this culture of the self was just abstract advice given by a few philosophers and technicians of the soul to a handful of disciples. We must not imagine that this concern with oneself was just a moral attitude. It was a widespread activity with a set of multifarious activities, techniques, and devices. Unfortunately, I don't have time to expand on this issue. I would just like to emphasize the importance of writing in the culture of the self as an example.[43] It is often assumed that personal writing is a modern

---

* As the text is obscure here, we have corrected this sentence using the manuscript.

discovery—maybe an innovation of the sixteenth century or the Reformation. In fact, the relation to oneself through writing has been a very long tradition in the West. I think it is possible to observe a shift from the culture of memory, which was still dominant in the Socratic attitude, to the practice of writing and taking notes in the culture of the Greco-Roman period. The culture of the self in this period entailed the use of personal notebooks called *hupomnēmata*. In these personal notebooks, you noted your readings, conversations, and themes for future meditation; you also wrote down your dreams and your daily schedule.

Writing letters was also important in these practices of the self, as in a letter you had to maintain a relationship to yourself and somebody else at the same time. This could be a director, friend, or somebody to whom you gave advice, valuable both for him and for yourself. At the same time, as these practices spread, it would seem the experience of the self, by virtue of this very fact, was intensified and widened. The self became a field of observations. Seneca and Pliny's letters and the correspondence between Marcus Aurelius and Fronto, demonstrate the vigilance and the meticulous attention one needed to pay to oneself. This attention often concerned the details of daily life, nuances of health and mood, the small physical malaises experienced, the movements of spirit, one's readings, remembered quotations, and reflections on particular events. A certain way of relating to oneself and a whole field of experience can be seen here that were absent in earlier documents.

From this point of view, Aelius Aristides's *Sacred Tales* are a remarkable testimony.[44] These texts written by Aelius Aristides are expressions of gratitude to Asclepius, the god of health. Aelius Aristides was in fact, sick for more than a decade, but what is interesting in this text, which is an expression of gratitude to the god who saved him, is that Aelius Aristides provides a transcription of hundreds and hundreds of dreams he had during that decade. This text, which in its original form was more than three hundred thousand lines long, is a real personal journal not only of Aelius Aristides's illness but of his everyday life, night and day. Within the traditional framework of gratitude to the god, Aelius Aristides provides an account of his illness, malaises, sufferings, diverse feelings, his premonitory dreams and dreams that offer advice, medicines that need to be tried, and so on. Do we reach the limits of hypochondria in this case? We most certainly do. But knowing the extent of Aelius Aristides's illness is not the problem. Rather, what is important is recognizing the means provided by the culture of his time that helped him formulate his personal experience of illness and convey this to others.

Forgive me for passing over all this so quickly. I wanted to suggest that the theme of concerning oneself with oneself during this period of the High Empire was not just to be found within one particular philosophical doctrine; it was a universal precept and also a real practice. Many individuals responded to this code. It was a practice that had its own institutions, rules, methods, techniques, and exercises. It was also a mode of experience, of individual experience but also a collective experience with its own means and forms of expression. That's the reason why I think we can speak of a culture of the self at this time.

In conclusion, I think we have to answer a legitimate question. If it is true, as I have just said, that the concern with oneself and all the techniques tied up with it were so important in classical culture, how is it that this theme has apparently disappeared, or seems to have disappeared? How is it, to put things very simply, that the memory of *gnōthi seauton* has been presented as one of the highest expressions of ancient thought while the other principle, *epimelē seautō*, "taking care of yourself," which was important for so long, has been forgotten? One can provide several reasons for this.[45] First, is the ethical paradox of Christian asceticism. In this kind of asceticism, the concern for the self takes the form of a sacrifice: the renunciation of the self is the major goal in the work we need to do on ourselves. The second reason is that, in our world, most of these techniques of the self have been integrated into educational and pedagogical, medical and psychological techniques. Techniques of the self have been embedded into either authoritarian or disciplinary structures, or they are replaced and transformed by public opinion, mass media, and polling techniques, which play a formative role in our attitude toward others and ourselves. So, the culture of the self is now imposed on people by others and has lost its independence. The third reason is, I think, that the human sciences assume that the main and major relationship to the self is, and needs to be, essentially a relationship of knowledge. The fourth and last reason is that most of the time people think that what we must do is disclose, liberate, and excavate the hidden reality of the self. But the self, I think, must be considered not as a reality that might be hidden; I think the self needs to be considered as the correlative of technologies built and developed throughout our history. The problem, then, is not to liberate and "free" the self but to consider how it could be possible to elaborate new types and new kinds of relationship to ourselves.[46]

DISCUSSION WITH THE
DEPARTMENT OF PHILOSOPHY

MICHEL FOUCAULT: Well you see, I can't give you a precise answer, because I am still working on this area and topic.* But what strikes me is that some, maybe most, or at least some historians of literature, have been interested in self-narration, self-description, and confession. Most of them have been interested in and have paid attention to the problem of the rhetorical structure of the narration of the self—the rhetorical structure that is implied in this kind of self-description. But what I am interested in—and I think this could be a worthwhile study in the field of literature—are the relations between this type of literature and the techniques you find in spiritual life either in the fields of philosophy or religion. Some studies, I think, have been made of this precise problem of the relation between spiritual techniques and literature in the sixteenth century. Techniques of self-examination in the Protestant churches and communities have been studied for example. But I don't think this has been the case for antiquity. It is very clear that the spiritual experience you find in well-known texts like the *Confessions* of Augustine was prepared by centuries of exercises of writing about oneself. For instance, a Christian writer at the end of the fourth century, Synesius, who is very typical of the relation between the Christian and Pagan culture of the time, wrote a very interesting book, a kind of handbook, on the interpretation of dreams.[47] At the beginning of this text there are some very exciting pages where he says that emperors have forbidden the use of magic and oracles and things like that. But, he says, it doesn't matter, because the oracle is inside yourself, and this oracle is the dream. So,

---

* The question was not recorded.

what you must do every morning is write down your dreams, keep this account with you, and read it again and again. You then have a permanent interpretation of what is going on inside you [...].* It's not just a manual of dream interpretation, but a manual for recording dreams. And you can find many other examples. What I mean is that this culture of the self was not just a philosophical idea, but it really was a practice, a social and an individual practice. I think people's experience of themselves through these techniques changed a lot in the course of the history of subjectivity. The kind of Christian literature you see developing at the beginning of the fourth century, people's narrations about themselves, their conversions, and their relations to God and so on was prepared by this history. This would be an interesting study, I think.

AUDIENCE: *When you quoted that text by Epicurus that says it's never too early and never too late to find yourself,*[48] *what struck me about that quote was Lacan, I think, talking about "the modern hero,"*[49] *for whom it's always too early and always too late. We should still talk about that, some sense of the on time always being not on time.*

Yes, this problem of being "on time" and not being on time as you know was one of the main problems in Greek ethics—the notion of kairos.[50] Kairos is the right moment. In the first Greek texts, the problem for ethics was choosing the right moment to do something. Why was this notion of kairos so important in the Greek ethics? I can't give you a very clear answer, but I can give you an example. In the ethics of sexual life, the problem was definitely not about knowing what kind of things you could do with your sexual partner. You cannot find anything about the kind of acts and pattern of sexual

---

* Several incomprehensible words.

behavior you should engage in with your partner in Greek literature. This was not the problem, neither was the sexual partner a problem. But they did have a lot of very strict rules surrounding sexual behavior, rules which dealt not with the sexual partner or the kind of behavior but with things like kairos, the right moment. In Plutarch, for instance, you find a several pages of discussion about the best moment of the day to have sex: before dinner, after dinner, during the day, during the night, at the end of the night, the beginning of the night, and so on.[51] Well, that's just one example. In general, I think the Greeks' problem was how to deal with necessity and fortune—Ananke and Tykhe. The Greeks had what you might call a very fatalistic attitude toward Ananke and Tykhe, as you know. Anyway, the problem faced by ethics, behavior, conduct, and politics was definitely not in trying to change things in relation to Ananke and Tykhe, but in dealing with them as they were and catching the right moment when you could actually do something. Kairos was the play, the element through which human freedom could deal with and manage Ananke, the world's necessity. That, I think, is the reason why kairos, the problem of the right moment, was one of the central problems in Greek ethics.

That's it for the Greeks. Turning now to Lacan. This is a good question, because the problem of psychoanalysis involves how to deal with the necessity of desire. I think that Lacan . . . sorry, I'm going back to the Greeks . . . In Greek medicine, as you know, the problem was not how to change anything in the nature of pathos, disease; the problem was choosing the right moment in the development of the crisis in order to act and then, either accept the issue and the outcome, or help the patient.[52] It was one of those moments [the doctor had to manage]. And I think in Lacan you find something like that in the role of the psychoanalyst in the process of desire. This isn't so far from the role of the Greek doctor—the psychoanalyst's role is to choose the right moment, the kairos. Well, I have at least developed some parallels, but I don't have anything very special to say about the problem of the right moment in Lacan, but they exist: psychoanalysis is an ethical technique far more [than a science*].[53]

Is there an institutional setting that allows the development of the self?

As you might recall, I never said that the individual had to develop himself. I have tried to show you the way the self is constituted. Relations to ourselves are constituted through a number of practices, techniques, which are characteristic of ethics. What is ethics? Ethics is, I think, the way individuals constitute themselves as moral subjects in their activity, their action, and so on.[54] So, the problem is not developing the self but determining what kind of relationship to yourself is able to establish you as an ethical subject. It is not the development of the self; it is the problem of constituting the self.

So, you're talking strictly about ethics and avoiding institutions?

Well, no, these practices of the self are linked to certain institutions. In Greek and Greco-Roman culture, in appearance there were no institutions, in the strict sense, intended to deal with this practice of the self. But in fact, you can find them easily in something like Epictetus's school, a real institution which Epictetus characterized as an *iatreion*, a dispensary.[55] This school was not a school where people learned syllogisms, literature, or grammar. They learned how to create a certain relation to themselves and were taught how to build this kind of relation. So, it was an institution for the formation and in-

---

* Conjecture; some words inaudible.

stitution of this relation. This institutionalization of the culture of the self, I think, has taken on very large and coercive dimensions in Christianity, through practices like confession, penance, and in modern society through things like the school system, the pedagogical system, educational institutions, and so on. And as you know only too well the penal system also has the same goal. One of its features, of course, is to constitute a certain type of self, as the criminal comes to recognize himself as a criminal through the penal system.

I'm just wondering what modern institutions and traditions would have to gain from talking about the self and techniques of helping one develop the self.

It's not a question of developing. You don't have to develop yourself. You need to constitute yourself as an ethical subject. That's not developing. The self is not a reality that is a given at the beginning which must develop in accordance with a certain pattern or model. The self is not a psychological reality, or maybe it becomes a psychological reality, or at least a matrix of experience through certain historico-cultural forms.[56]

You said that, in contrast to the moderns, for the ancients the problem was not discovering one's true self but mastery of the self. But when the Stoics sought to overcome illusions and passions which they assimilated with false opinions, how can their approach be distinguished from a discovery of the self? Could you expand on that distinction?

Yes, you're quite right. What I said concerning this difference was somewhat holistic. In fact, getting rid of people's illusions about themselves was a real problem for the Stoics. But when you look at the Stoic texts on this problem, you see that when they try to make it clear what the self really is the criterion is what is dependent on me and what is independent of me in the world and what is around me. I can exercise my sovereignty in the domain that is dependent on me. But I can't change what is independent from me, that is not me, and I need to be free of it, or at least quite indifferent to it. So, you can see that there is an attempt, an effort, a work of discovering the self in Stoic discourse. But this work of discovery is only the allocation of what is dependent on and what is independent from me. The problem is defining exactly what the domain of my sovereignty is.[57] I think you see something very different with Christianity. For the Christian, the problem becomes the illusions I have about myself that prevent me from knowing exactly what is going on inside me. When I have a desire and am not able to recognize this desire as such, then I am the victim of an illusion. I'll give you a very simple example from Cassian. It concerns the regulations that apply to the life of Eastern monks. To provide an example of these kinds of regulations, Cassian cites the case of a young monk who was very holy, or at least very anxious to achieve holiness. He wanted to fast much more and for much longer than the other monks. In appearance, this was a very good project and he sincerely thought that it was in itself a good initiative and a good desire to have. But his director showed him that, in fact, if he wanted to fast longer than the others, it was not because he wanted to arrive more quickly at holiness but because he wanted to be praised by the others. It was not a sign of holiness but the movement of an impure desire. It was not a suggestion from God, it was a suggestion from Satan.[58] Since you can have the interior illusion that a suggestion from Satan can take the shape and form of a suggestion from God, then you need to interpret your ideas and representations, desires, and so on. This is the new obligation of the hermeneutics of the self.[59] This hermeneutics of the self is, I think, something quite different from the problem of what is dependent on me and what is independent of me.[60]

I was wondering if you could explain exactly what you mean by "the self?"

The self is nothing other than the relation to the self. The self is a relation. The self is not a reality, it's not something structured that is a given at the beginning. It is a relation to the self.[61] I think that it is impossible to give a definition of the self other than *this* relation and this set of relations.

What do you mean by the culture of the self? Are you using culture in the sense of "cultured" or in a broader sense?

Well, the first question was about the self and this second question is about culture. The second answer is, I think, somewhat easier and longer than the first. When I used the word "culture," I wanted to show, I have tried to show, first, that the culture of the self means the formation of certain relations to oneself, and in the case of Greco-Roman culture, this formation of the self takes the form of mastery and sovereignty. So first, it's a notion. Second point, it is a set of techniques. The self builds these relations, and to do this, you need to engage in exercises, like meditation, reading books, writing [...],* and so on and so forth. Third, the culture of these relations to the self and techniques of the relation to the self imply, produce, or induce a type of concrete experience of yourself. When you compare, for instance, Cicero's letters written at the end of the Roman Republic and the letters written [a century]† later by Seneca, and of course Marcus Aurelius and Fronto's letters, you can see the landscape is quite different. The way people spoke about themselves, what interested them about themselves, what was pertinent to their experience of themselves was quite, quite different. That's the third thing. Fourth, these relations to the self were not just something personal and in-

---

* A few inaudible words.

† Conjecture; partially inaudible passage.

dividual. I have mentioned there were schools, treatises, you could read and write about those relations, and people related to each other about themselves. For instance, Seneca and Lucilius exchanged letters about themselves for years and years. So, it is a social activity. These four elements, a notion, a practice, a type of experience, and a social activity, and I could also add all the books, literature, philosophy, and other things that deal with this—all this, I think, constitutes the culture of the self. I don't think the word "culture" is excessive [*exagéré*] here.

Could you elaborate on what you mean by the cultural importance of writing in relation to the practices of the self in a society that was inherently illiterate?

First point: what I have said about the culture of the self is, of course, only pertinent to the social classes that were the bearers of culture. And of course, I am not speaking about slaves, because in Greco-Roman society some slaves were literate. But from a quantitative point of view, most of the people who lived in the Greco-Roman world had nothing to do with this culture of the self. But there weren't many who were illiterate, [. . .]* among the privileged social classes. The Athenian citizens of the fourth century could all read and write. Of course, citizens made up only a part of the inhabitants of Athens. But they were rather numerous, and all of them could read and write. From this point of view, they were much more literate than seventeenth century society in Europe, for instance. That's the second point.

You asked me about the importance of writing. Well, I think that we can say this. In the fourth century BC, the main form of the culture of the self was memory. Memory meant that people had to learn a certain number of precepts, verses, lines,

---

* A few inaudible words.

and aphorisms by heart. These were called *gnōmē*,[62] which were both truths and rules, rules of behavior which took the form of concise truths and eternal truths uttered by poets, philosophers, and sages. The Socratic lessons and of course Platonic philosophy, I think, were mainly oriented toward the importance of memory as the principal form of the relation to yourself.[63] You arrived at the relation to yourself by getting through those precepts learned by heart, and that you could concentrate in your memory and get . . .

I'm wondering if you would allow an alternative, nonliterary way of constituting the self through codified images or exemplary behavior for example?

Yes, of course. In Greek and Roman society, examples had an important role. But where do you look for those examples? In texts, narratives, and books. I don't think you can offer examples as an alternative to literary culture.

But didn't there exist other nonliterate ways of constituting the self, for example through an exemplary person, the cult of the saint?

Of course. I am not denying this, but I thought that you were setting literature and examples up as alternatives in Greek culture. In Greek mainstream culture, the example is one of the main themes, it is not [an alternative to literature].* And of course, in the case of the self and the culture of the self, you have this kind of nonliterary way of constituting yourself.

Certain movements that have taken place in the United States in the last decade, such as punk music and an interest in Eastern religion, have been considered by people—most notably Christopher Lasch[64]—as an attempt to escape from history and its consequences. Do you think these attempts to discover oneself in the

---

* Conjecture; a few inaudible words.

last decades can be characterized in this way? Must the search for self inevitably be an attempt to escape from the world around us in order to achieve it?

[First point] as you know and may have noticed, I've never used the word "narcissism." I don't think the relations to the self are related to narcissism. The second point is that these very striking movements in the States also exist in other societies [. . .].* I don't really understand what you mean by an effort to escape history. These movements are a part of history. They are a part of your history. And I think this effort to establish new relations to the self in different forms is now quite common. What educational and political, indeed all systems, are proposing is not satisfying people as they try to organize, build, and determine the relation to themselves. So, we are looking for something else. This mismatch between the kind of relationship to the self proposed by political parties and educational systems and [the relation people wish to have with themselves]† is a part of history, I think. You don't escape your history when you engage in this; you make history. What you are escaping, or trying to escape, is a certain model of the relation to yourselves that has been presented to you as the best possible model.

You spoke of the erotic relation between master and student in Greek culture, and I was wondering if you could address the role of eroticism in the culture of the self in history.

What I said earlier was that when I started studying, or claiming to study, the history of sexuality, I did not know and was not aware that the problem, the main problem, in the history of sexuality, is not the problem of desire and the repres-

---

* A few inaudible words.
† Conjecture; a few inaudible words.

sion of desire. [Instead] I found the constitution of the self is for a large part determined by the way people relate to their own sexuality, at least in our societies, and perhaps in other societies. [. . .]* In our societies the relation to the self is constituted in large part within the field of sexual experience. This is not an answer, but I think it is quite impossible to dissociate the problem of the constitution of the self and the problem of the history of sexuality. We are sexual beings and our selves are constituted through our experience of sexuality.[65] This sounds like something psychoanalysts might say perhaps [. . .].† But what I would say is that if psychoanalysis is able to define the self through sexuality, it is because it is in fact through this experience of sexuality that the relation to the self has been and is constituted in our society.

How has the master-student role in contemporary society changed since the ancient Greeks?

Well, I wouldn't say that the relationship between a master or a teacher and a pupil is sexual in Greek society. As you know, you find the first philosophical and ethical definition of complete sexual abstinence in Greek culture in relation to boys and the love of boys, and the love of teachers for boys.[66] It we look at Christian asceticism—the so-called renunciation of the flesh, body, sex, and sexual pleasure—the same theme was shared by the Greeks, not in relation to women or sex in general but in relation to boys. That's the paradox most historians refuse to see in relation to this famous Greek homosexuality—namely the fact that in Greek society, where sexual relations between men, or at least between boys and

---

* A few inaudible words.
† Partially inaudible passage.

men were free, it was in *this* society that you find the first formulation of complete sexual renunciation in the West.

You spoke of norms in Discipline and Punish, *and you said that what distinguishes the norms in our society is that they're linked to rationality—that is, we do things because they are something we know will be good for us. Would you say that what makes norms in our society special is that they are linked to biopower? Is there a certain relationship between rationality and norms that is important?*

You are asking me about the Aufklärung, am I right? I'd say norms exist in every society. There is no society which only has laws, [you have the juridical system]* and norms. But I think— and this was emphasized in the book you mentioned—you can see the intervention of a normative system in what was traditionally, and still is, the juridical system. In our society, our juridical system—at least the penal and civil systems— cannot function without an explicit and permanent reference to norms. To take a very simple example, the penal system [*système pénal*] cannot function without referring to madness, normal behavior, mental illness, and so on.[67] This interface between the juridical system and a normative system is not something we are able to organize into a noncontradictory or homogeneous system at present. This heterogeneity of the normative system and of the legal system is, I think, the source of many difficulties for several of our practices.

Would you prefer to say that the norms linked to the juridical system should be the object of a certain theory about what we should do to better ourselves, what would be good for us?

No, definitely not. I think that norms are something else. Norms are not the rules that are used to analyze behavior.

---

* Conjecture; passage difficult to hear.

DISCUSSION WITH THE
DEPARTMENT OF HISTORY

AUDIENCE: *The first question I'd like to put to you concerns the shift in the methodological focus of your work from your earlier archaeological perspective to what you have described in the essay that you wrote on Nietzsche as a genealogical perspective.*[68] *Is this a significant and radical break in your work, or can we conceive of genealogy as basically similar to archaeology, merely moving from discourse to power and to apparatuses that are outside discourse? How would you describe the difference between archaeology and genealogy as a historical method?*

MICHEL FOUCAULT: This a good question and a difficult one. I provided these two words with very different meanings to indicate two different sets of problems. When I used the term "archaeological research," I wanted to differentiate what I was doing from social history since I didn't want to analyze society but the facts of discourses. I also wanted to dissociate this analysis of discourses from philosophical hermeneutics—that is, from interpretations of what has been said by deciphering something that hadn't been said. When I used the term "archaeological research," I wanted to say that I was dealing with a set of discourses which needed to be analyzed as an event or a set of events. Something had been said, particular things had been said and discursive events of this kind are events like any other events, but they have a special status and particular effects that are not the same as economic events, battles, or demographic changes or things like that. That's what I mean by "archaeology"—it is the methodological framework of my analysis.

By "genealogy" I mean the reason for, and the goal of, analyzing these discourses as events. What I am trying to show is how these discursive events have, in a certain way, determined what constitutes our present and ourselves. This can include our knowledge, practices, type of rationality, our relationship to ourselves and others. That's what genealogy is. So, I would say that genealogy is the goal of the analysis, and archaeology is the material and methodological framework.[69]

Would it then be fair to say that, whereas archaeology stresses the discontinuities between various discourses or epistemes, genealogy is much more interested in the subtle continuities and the ways in which the present is in a sense anticipated by the past?

I wouldn't say that exactly. The general theme of my research is the history of thought.[70] How can we undertake the history of thought? Thought cannot be dissociated from discourses of course, and in any case we don't have access to thought, either to our present thought, our own thought, the thought of our contemporaries, or that of previous periods. We can only have access to thought through discourses. This is what makes archaeological study necessary. It has nothing to do with continuity or discontinuity and you can find both continuity and discontinuity in those discourses. For instance, when I am looking at the history of sexual ethics now, I am obliged to recognize that you find exactly the same formulations concerning sexual ethics from the fourth century BC right up until now. The theory of marriage, of faithfulness, and so on is the same, at least it is from the first century AD.[71] So you have continuity. But you find discontinuity in other systems of discourses, for instance in scientific discourses. What's very striking in our culture and in this archaeological research is finding continuity in certain fields like ethics that lasts for centuries and millennia. But in science, you find some very rapid changes, such drastic changes that when you read a medical book written at the beginning of the eighteenth century for example, you often cannot figure out what they are talking about and what kind of disease they are referring to. This is very difficult, and you need multiple translations to understand what they are talking about, the kind of disease, and so on. But if you look at a book written at the beginning of the nineteenth century, after Bichat, Laennec, and others, even if you recognize that everything is wrong, you clearly recognize what they are talking about, and you can tell whether it's true or not. As for most of the books written up until the eighteenth century and the middle of the eighteenth century, you can't tell whether they are wrong or not, because they really make no sense to us from a medical point of view.[72] So in this case you have a very drastic change and a real discontinuity. But this is definitely not a universal principle.

One of the most frequent critical responses to your work in America concerns the curious lack of explanation for change in the archaeological method. Things just seem to replace one another, and you are generally less concerned with why they replace one another than with the mere fact of the replacement. Does your genealogical method pay more attention to the sources of changes, to the reasons why things have radically changed or remained the same, or is this still an issue that is essentially bracketed in your work and not one of your central concerns?

I am aware I haven't been clear enough about this problem of discontinuity, which doesn't have a lot of importance for me. I remember reading a very short notice about myself—one line—which was my name, "philosopher of discontinuity." Something that struck me, and really nobody since has shown me that I was wrong on this, is that when you look at the history of at least some sciences from the end of the sixteenth century to the beginning of the nineteenth century, you see very important changes in medicine, natural history, economics, and other disciplines. I am leaving aside the problem of physics and chemistry, where you can find, I think exactly the same very dramatic changes. These are facts. You could try to reduce or explain these facts by invoking some kind of change in society and so on. I have never read any pertinent explanations anywhere of these dramatic scientific changes through correlative, parallel, and similar changes in society. Nobody has ever convinced me that the changes in capitalist society from the sixteenth to the beginning of the nineteenth century are a good explanation for the change from natural history in the sixteenth century to biology in the nineteenth. I think that scientific thought has a type of historicity—I don't know whether this word means anything in English—a type of historicity and a way of changing, that is quite specific with the possibility of changing nearly everything at the same moment. Rather, I'd say not just the possibility but the necessity. One of the main characteristics of scientific thought is that it is a coherent system of thought, so that when something is changed at a certain point, you are obliged to change other things. And, of course, there are several levels of change. Sometimes only a concept changes, sometimes a theory, sometimes a model, as Kuhn describes.[73] At other times, more than a model changes—nearly everything changes: the objects, theory, field, type of rationality, models, and concepts. You sometimes find these dramatic changes in the history of science involving nearly everything, the field, the objects, the type of rationality. For instance, you can look at the history of genetics in the mid-nineteenth century and the genetics still used by Darwin, one of the founders of modern science. But the genetics he used is completely foreign to our [contemporary] genetics. But after Mendel and De Vries at the end of the nineteenth and the beginning of the twentieth centuries, you have not just a change in model but the appearance of a new field of research. In the thirty years between Mendel and De Vries, you have a dramatic change. It is not revolutions, the development of industries, or imperialism which can be accused of or credited with the rise of genetics. It was something that had nothing to do with this type of historicity.

I was interested in dealing with these changes in one of my books, *The Order of Things*,[74] where I tried to show how some empirical sciences developed in the seventeenth and eighteenth centuries through dramatic change with no external explanation, or at least I don't know of anyone who has been able to give me an external explanation. But I am certainly not rejecting these kinds of explanation on principle—and my apologies for talking about myself, but you asked. In the book on madness,[75] I tried to show how a certain situation, a certain relation to madness or at least to mad people changed between the sixteenth century and the beginning of the eighteenth century. These changes were determined by a number of social processes, including the development of an industrial society, the unemployment crisis, and the problem of the unemployed in the seventeenth century. These were the reasons why the great general hospitals were constructed. All of this forms the social context which allows you to understand, not why particular scientific theories were developed around madness, but why madness became a problem at a certain moment. I think it's worth emphasizing that there is a difference between explaining the change in a scientific model and rationality, and I don't think the change in a scientific rationality can be explained through social processes. But I think the fact that something becomes a scientific problem and emerges as a problem society must deal with can be explained by social processes, and I think this applies in the case of madness. Or again, why disease and physical illness became such a social problem at the end of the eighteenth century that they were obliged to organize those large hospitals. The reasons were obviously social, economic and demographic with the development of urbanism and towns and epidemics. All that was the reason why disease and physical illness became a huge social and political problem.[76] You can see the effects of the rise of this problem in very important books such as the French book about . . . What's it called? *Medicine* . . . or the eight-volume German work about the politics of health—sorry, I can't remember the titles.[77] Anyway—these books were one of the major signs of the emergence of illness—physical illness—as a social and political problem for all of society. But when, a few years later, Bichat used a certain type of rationality to analyze certain symptoms, you can't situate it through the analysis of social processes.

So, you never stopped doing archaeology?

No, I never stopped doing archaeology, and I never stopped doing genealogy. Genealogy defines the aim and purpose of the work, and archaeology indicates the field I deal with in order to construct a genealogy.

Could you tell us a little about why history as a profession became important in France at the end of the nineteenth century?

I have a student who is working in this field.[78] My idea was that the development of historical studies became very important in France toward the end of the seventeenth century and at the beginning of the eighteenth, when the aristocracy and the monarchy came into competition over the foundations of their own rights. Was monarchy just the expression of an aristocratic social structure, or was monarchy something that had its roots in the nation, in the third estate [*tiers état*] and the bourgeoisie? This was a very important problem. At the end of the seventeenth and the beginning of the eighteenth century,

when the great administrative monarchy of Louis XIV began
to decline, you find a real explosion of historical research.
This research was both juridical and historical, and the link
between these two forms is very clear.[79] So that was my hypothesis, which I discussed with the student, but she has now
found something else. She found that scholarly research done
by the monks and the Benedictines at the beginning of the
seventeenth century seems to have been the most important
roots of [historical research]. This was done of course, in the
climate of the Counter-Reformation, and it's very interesting
to see. This is only an outline and much too simplistic—but we
could say that for the Reformation, the problem was getting
back to the first text, to *the* text. Historical research on this text
was of course important for [the Protestants], but the problem of hermeneutics was much more important. How was
this text to be interpreted, since it was *the* text and a meaning
needed to be found for it in the present? This is the problem of
hermeneutics. The problem for the Counter-Reformation and
Catholics was quite different. It was a matter of finding and
justifying a historical continuity from early Christianity until
the present, and to provide the juridical foundation and the
historical justification, for this continuity. So, you can see the
outline, the kind of split between the hermeneutic orientation
typical of the Reformation and historical justification typical
of Catholicism. This could be a hypothesis. . . .

*Should we look at techniques of writing history to understand
the transformations you are talking about? For example, I am
thinking of the appearance of the notion of the century as a temporal unit which appeared in the sixteenth century and which profoundly modified the way history was written.*

Yes, certainly. For example, we have the problem of collect-
ing sources, which is very important and directly related to

this problem of constituting a continuity. Catholics and the Counter-Reformation started to collect all the documents that could justify a continuity due to the conflict of the Reformation. The great collections of patristic literature started at the beginning of the seventeenth century for instance. This wasn't exactly a technique of writing, but it was a technique of collection, which is something incredibly important. Of course, the problem of writing itself, the problem of chronicles and the problem of administrative archives, were also very important. The great project of administrative archival science started in the seventeenth century. All that is incredibly important. What I would describe as temporal techniques were developed— namely, the technical and material conditions surrounding the development of historical knowledge.

In Discipline and Punish, *you talk about criminal law and the prison system as a way of talking about disciplinary society, even if you also discussed other subjects, like welfare or education. I'm wondering if it's right to think that criminal law and the prison system have a special role in the historical development of disciplinary society, and whether they will continue to have an important or a special role?*

First of all, what I wanted to say in this book on the prison was not that the disciplinary society starts with the development of prisons. I would say exactly the contrary. The problem that struck me when I was studying this field was that when you read the books written by eighteenth-century reformers and social reformers, you notice a very strong and aggressive reaction to any system of imprisonment. There was a very simple reason for this: The prison, at least in the French, Italian, and German systems—the English one was a little different— was not a punishment; it was an administrative measure with regards to people outside the law, outside the juridical system and institutions. It was resorted to only when the administration or the sovereign power wanted to get rid of somebody— they put them in jail. So, jail was the exact opposite of what people were looking for when they wanted to build or come up with a new and effective system of penal justice. Criticism of the prison was general in the mid-eighteenth century. But when you look at what happened and was organized and institutionalized at the end of the eighteenth century by the new penal codes in France, in Germany, and elsewhere, you find the prison everywhere. It became the principal and main means of punishment. Why this change? This was my problem and this is the theme of the book.[80] I have the feeling the reason for this was that although prison was the symbol of the arbitrary power of the monarchy, in spite of this, prison and imprisonment were found to be a very good means and tool not just for punishing but also for reforming prisoners and inmates. How was it imagined that this reform, this change of minds, attitudes, and behaviors could be achieved? Through disciplinary techniques. And where were those disciplinary techniques to be found? In the school and the army, where they had been in use since the mid-seventeenth century. They tried to build penal institutions using the model of the school and the army, not the model of the former prison. And so, you can see the penal system as an expression or a consequence, one of the final consequences, of this disciplinary system which had been developed in other institutions.[81] This final application of the disciplinary system then became a model for a new development of disciplinary techniques in other fields. Bentham's panopticon was very interesting from this point of view, because Bentham came up with the idea of the panopticon as a way of organizing a good prison, a good prison where people could be treated, trained and reformed in a disciplinary institution. From there, he came up with the idea of also using this panopticon for factories, schools, and so on.[82] So you can see how this developed.

So, prison is only a part of this disciplinary system. When I use the term "disciplinary systems," I don't mean that society has been organized according to this model. What I term a disciplinary system is much more a kind of rationality than a total institution. This is different from what Goffman describes— that is, real institutions with a certain kind of internal organization.[83] What I mean by a disciplinary system is much more a kind of rationality. How can we govern other people, train and get them to behave in a certain way? What is the best, most economical, and efficient way of doing this? It's discipline, I think. But after a while, and more than a century of applying this disciplinary system, people noticed that it was by no means the most economical means but was very costly; that there were much more efficient, discreet, and implicit ways of informing and leading people. To give you just one example: When you see how large factories were organized in France at the beginning of the eighteenth century, you can clearly see they used a model of disciplinary rationality with general oversight and very strict rules. This was to the point that in the second half of the eighteenth century, the government proposed using soldiers as miners in large mines in France and transforming miners into soldiers. This was because they considered the army to be a good disciplinary organization and the working class ought to be organized as an army, so as to be efficient and docile. But by the mid-nineteenth century or even by the 1820s and 1830s, you can see clearly that it was no longer seen as a good method of creating docile workers but that a system based on insurance, savings banks, and so on was seen to be much more efficient than military discipline.

A new kind of control and organization developed from this moment, that we could describe as a system of control using insurance, which is quite different and much more efficient and acceptable than the disciplinary system.

Just to clarify what you're saying then, if someone wanted to do a study of disciplinary techniques, they would not start with the prison system.

No. The disciplinary system is, I think, a type, technique, and technology that is very specific to a certain period. You can now find other much more sophisticated means of making people behave in a particular way. The disciplinary system is not efficient. I'll give you an example. Even in the army, which has always been the focus and cradle of disciplinary techniques, disciplinary techniques have changed a lot. In one of the most efficient armies in the world—I am referring to the Israeli army—disciplinary techniques are very limited compared to the disciplinary techniques that were still in place in armies in World War I.

In the lecture you contrasted two models of the self: one the Platonic model linked to the question of origin, memory, and to depths to be discovered and a model that anticipated the Freudian hermeneutics of the self; and the other, a Stoic model which was turned not toward memory but toward the future and toward death. Was this second model simply an exteriorization of what was internal in the first, or is it a matter of something else entirely?

This isn't an easy question to answer. When I contrasted Plato's relation to the self, or the kind of relation to the self that was described in that very strange dialogue which is the *Alcibiades* to the Stoic one, I wasn't setting them up as internal versus external. I would say virtually the contrary. The Neoplatonists considered the *Alcibiades*, which is not typical of Platonic philosophy, as the first Platonic text that needed to be studied as an entry into Platonic doctrine, but in fact it's a very strange text. In this text, Plato, at least when he is analyzing the notion of taking care of oneself, says that Alcibiades needed to take care of himself because he had to rule others or wanted to rule others as a political leader. First point. [Second, Plato said] that to take care of himself he had to know what he was. What he was meant by this was he had to know his soul. And how can we know our soul, unless we contemplate it in its essential element, in its divine element? This is not exactly an internal relationship to oneself, since to know yourself, you must look at divinity or the divine element, you have to turn your eyes toward the light, the supercelestial light. So, you must move away from what is closest to you, your body, your everyday life and sensations in order to go beyond the world—it is then that you discover what you are. So, you see, it's not an internal relation, even if memory is very important, but it is a memory that leads you to something other than your immediate world.[84]

In the case of the Stoics, it's not an external relation. Of course, death is important to the Stoics and you need to hurry, not exactly to die, but to be ready to die. As you know well, the Stoic ideal was to live every day of your life as if it were your last.[85] There is a very interesting section in one of Seneca's letters where he says that the day is a reduced version of the year—morning is spring, noon is summer, and so on—and that the year is a reduced version of life, spring is childhood, summer is youth, which is a Pythagorean idea. Well, anyway, you have those correspondences. Seneca says you must live every day as if it were a year and you must also live every day as if it were your whole life. Every morning, you must recognize yourself as a child and know that evening will be your old age and that you must be ready to die at the end of the day.[86]

It's not exactly an anticipation of death, it's not an attitude of turning from the past with memory to the future with death. It is a way of looking at your life as if it were complete. It is to have your whole life under your gaze and to have a kind of perception of your life as an act of memorization. For Stoicism, I think, this anticipation of death was a kind of memorization and integration of whatever events occurred in your life. So, you see, it is not exactly an opposition between external and internal. It marks a very important change but not exactly that one.

What other definitions does this other type of self you have just described link up to now?

Well, what I wanted to show—but of course this was rather difficult in a short lecture—is that the kind of attention the Stoics wanted people to pay to themselves in relation to what they were doing and the accordance between what they needed to do and what they actually did, all that started a new kind of relationship to oneself, a kind of permanent attention, but for the Stoics, the problem was definitely not discovering or deciphering what people really were. The problem of what they were was not in the least important. The problem was whether the things they were doing during the day were in accordance with the law or not. But it was, I think, a first step toward a new kind of relationship, which became very important in Christianity, with people looking at and examining themselves and what they had done every day and every evening. They started to ask the question, Can I recognize the reality of myself through the things I have been doing and ideas I have had during the day? Can I recognize the real desires and the real degree of purity of my soul? The problem for Christians was attaining a degree of purity that would allow them to be saved. The problem [of the relations] between purity, salvation, and the interpretation and deciphering of the self was, I think, important and something you don't find in the Stoics. For the Stoics the question was not one of purity but of conformity. The problem was not salvation in another world but perfection in this world. So, you can see in this Stoic relationship to oneself a kind of preparation for Christianity. The technique of the examination of the self was a Stoic technique that was used in the Christian monastery, and you find the description of the evening self-examination, in Seneca, in the third book of *De Ira* [*On Anger*].[87] In appearance, it's exactly the same formula as the one used in Christianity right up until the present day. But in fact, I think the questions Seneca asked himself were rather different. Anyway, you can find this technique in monastic institutions from the fourth and the beginning of the fifth centuries onward. You find this technique in Saint Benedict, but with, I think, a different aim, an aim which has been displaced, it is not exactly the same. The aim is to try and recognize the degree of purity of the soul in remembering the deeds of the day.

In your lecture you started out with the Greek and the Christian ideas of the culture of the self, and then toward the end you said that there might be new technologies and different ways in which people could take care of themselves now. Do you think perhaps that this culture of the self has always been going on, and we're just finding new ways of taking care of ourselves, or perhaps we're losing some of that capability of looking at ourselves, or even as some people say here, especially in California, that we look at ourselves too much?

I think what is most striking in Greco-Roman culture is the fact that they had something which seemed to be a real autonomous culture of the self. When I say "autonomous," I don't mean that it had no social, political, or cultural relations with

anything else but that people, or at least some of them in the
upper classes of course, decided, to take care of themselves.
Just as some people now can decide to cultivate themselves
by visiting art exhibitions and so on. It was definitely not a
question of an obligation founded on authority, they were not
obliged to do this, but it was something that was proposed as
important and valuable, something that would give them the
capacity to attain a better and a more beautiful life, a new type
of existence. So you see, it was a question of personal choice—
that's the first point. The second thing was that this culture of
the self was not related to religion at all. But when I say, "not
at all," this is much too simplistic—of course, there were relations, and the role of the Pythagoreans and Pythagoreanism
was very important. As you know, Pythagoreanism was both
a kind of religion and a philosophy, it was a mixture of philosophy and religion. For instance, even if in his youth Seneca
had some links with the Pythagoreans, Seneca didn't do what
he did for religious reasons. Plutarch on the other hand was
very religious in the sense that he practiced traditional rituals,
but when he took care of himself, it was for personal reasons.
The techniques of the self were not embedded in religious,
political, or even educational institutions. That's what I mean
by "autonomous." That's the second point. These practices
of the self were independent of pedagogical, religious, and
social institutions. The third thing is that this culture of the
self had its own literature and recipes as it were. For instance,
people wrote letters to each other with good recipes and techniques for taking care of themselves and they wrote treatises.
Plutarch sent his *Peri euthumias*, *On Tranquility of Mind*, to his
friend Fundanus,[88] who was a rather important Roman sen-
ator and political figure. He said to Fundanus, "Well, I know
you need this treatise which includes some considerations on

euthymia right now," Nobody knows, or at least I don't know, Fundanus's personal reasons for needing this advice—but Plutarch says, "I know you are in a hurry, that it's an emergency, and you need some considerations on *euthumia*, but I don't have time to write a special treatise for you. So I am sending you my personal notes on *euthymia*."[89] This was because he had a notebook where he had written advice, considerations, quotations, and examples relating to *euthymia*, and it is those personal notes, his personal notebook, he is supposed at least, to have sent to Fundanus. So, you can see a small world of techniques, notions, practices, and so on circulated between people, and that's what I mean by the autonomous existence of the culture of the self.

You used the word "technology." I know that can mean different things, many people say it does a lot of good, and allows people to do a lot of things, but then there are other people who say yes, but there are all the kids who sit in front of the TV set and never know what it is to think for themselves or write . . .

What I said at the end of the lecture was much too brief. This autonomy, the autonomous culture of the self, disappeared in a way after the development of Christianity, since the formation of the self and the way people needed to take care of themselves became embedded in religious, social, and educational institutions. Christian confession is very interesting from this point of view, since, in a way, confessing means examining yourself, remembering your deeds and sins, and recounting them to a priest and undertaking penance.[90] All of this was a way of having a relationship to yourself of course. First, this technique became necessary and obligatory, something people had to perform every year at least, then every month, then every week, and if you were a monk, every day. This is the first point. Second, you needed to confess to somebody who was imposed on you as a director; you had no choice. In the decree [*décret*] of 1215 which made confession obligatory in Christianity, you had to confess to the parish priest of your village and nobody else. Third, you had to answer a set of questions which were always the same, and most of the time it was the priest who asked the questions—"Did you do that? Did you do that? Did you do that?"—and set the penance. So you see, this is a way of taking care of yourself, and a way of letting somebody else take care of you. You could say the same of the educational system where the problem of the constitution of the self is very important. So, there was a care of the self, but it was not the form of autonomous culture you find in Greco-Roman society.

You said in the lecture that the classical culture of the self was quite different from the modern culture of the self. Nonetheless, can you see a continuity between the two or has the classical culture of the self completely disappeared?

Always the same questions! Please excuse me—I had a very interesting discussion with Paul [Rabinow] this morning and he asked me the same kind of question. What strikes me, is that before I came here, this question hadn't occurred to me. I have nearly finished my book and I didn't foresee this difficulty or this question . . . Paul made me aware of what wasn't clear in my exposé or my book. It's not a matter of presenting a golden age where everything was okay and people had the leisure to take care of themselves, a time far removed from Christianity, bourgeois society, industrial pressure, bad environments, and so on. No, it's not like that at all. I think it's also possible to show how hard, difficult, and perhaps terrible, the sexual ethics of antiquity could be. It's only a dream, perhaps a Hegelian or an Enlightenment dream, that Greek society was a golden age where the beautiful totality of life was aware of itself. There was no beautiful totality. But, I think, it is important to remember that in our present society our ethics and morals have been linked to religion for centuries. They are also linked to civil laws and a type of juridical organization. At a certain moment morality took the form of a kind of juridical structure—think [of] Kant. As you also know, ethics has been linked to science, that is to medicine, psychology, psychoanalysis, and even sociology. The three great reference points for our ethics—religion, law, and science are now, I think, worn out and spent. We are fully aware that we need an ethics, and that we cannot ask religion, law, or science to provide us with this ethics. We have the example of a society, Greco-Roman society, where an ethics, and a very important system of ethics, existed without these three references. This ethics is so important that part of our Christian, or so-called Christian, ethics comes from there. It is certainly not a matter of returning to Greco-Roman ethics, since a part of our own ethics already comes from there. But we know it's possible to research ethics, to build a new ethics, to create a place for what I would call the ethical imagination without any reference to religion, law, or science. That's the reason why I think the analysis of Greco-Roman ethics as an *aesthetics* of existence might be interesting.[91]

Are the practices of self-care and self-knowledge we have now inextricably linked to discipline?

I can't answer that directly because I am not sure. But I would say that at the very beginning the care of the self was something quite different from discipline. I would also say that discipline, at least the very intense discipline you find in eighteenth-century armies, in the Prussian army and also in the French and English armies, has nearly nothing to do with the care of the self, it is something that deals with behavior, the body and attitudes, and so on. It's very different. But it's a fact that at certain times there have been links between techniques of the care of the self and disciplinary techniques. For instance, in the monasteries and monastic institutions in the Middle Ages, you find very interesting relationships between the care of the self and discipline particularly in the Benedictine institutions. As you know, Benedictine monastic institutions were derived directly from the Roman legion and the Roman army. This monastic organization took the Roman legion as a model, with decurions and so on. They tried to use both this disciplinary model as well as techniques of the self that had been developed in the eastern asceticism of Evagrius Ponticus—where there was a spirituality that had nothing to do with the army. Also, let's take seventeenth to eighteenth-century Jesuit pedagogical institutions. Here you can see a very interesting relationship and link between the care of the self and disciplinary techniques. It is very interesting to see, the relationship between these two things in the eighteenth century in the great colleges, in the French sense of the word "college" as public institutions for boys.

In Discipline and Punish *and* The Will to Know *you have described how power operates, and that power operates from the top down and the bottom up, and you also say that power—rather power relations—are everywhere. I wonder if it's correct to think that the main source of resistance to power relations and possibly of the liberation that's supposed to follow is the pursuit of bodily pleasure.*

I am not sure I can answer this question. One thing that struck me when I was reading books on sexuality and psychoanalysis several years ago is the fact that people seem to be so uncomfortable when they speak about pleasure. The literature about desire is incredible, thousands of volumes have been devoted to desire, to the theory of desire, the repression of desire, and so on, but when people come to speaking about pleasure, they seem to go mute.[92] When you compare this to Greco-Roman literature on the same problems: sex, ethics, and so on, you can see that they really made no distinction, or almost no distinction, between *epithumia* and *hēdonē*. You always see the same formula recurring in these texts: either to be slave of *epithumiōn kai hēdonōn* or to be free from *epithumiōn kai hēdonōn*. Desire and pleasure form an entity that can't be dissociated. As you know well, talking about pleasure is seen as rather vulgar in psychoanalytical literature, and to be a really sophisticated psychoanalyst you need to talk about desire. There is an underevaluation of pleasure which is very striking in this kind of literature. Anyway, one of my aims in studying the techniques of the self is understanding how and why the problem of desire became so important, given that both desire and pleasure were such an important problem in Greco-Roman antiquity.[93] The problem in Greco-Roman antiquity was, What do we do with our pleasure? How do we experience this pleasure? To what extent, and within which limits? and so on. It was really a problem of pleasure and the use of pleasure. I haven't read any of the Chinese books about the erotic arts, but I have read books about them—for example, the very interesting book written by Van Gulik.[94] I don't know if you've read it, but it is very, very interesting. There you can see that the problem was not the problem of desire at all. The problem for the Chinese erotic arts was the problem of pleasure: how to experience pleasure, with what intensity, and so on.[95] I think we are a civilization, maybe the only civilization, where the problem of desire has become much more important than the problem of pleasure. What's the reason for this? Why do we recognize ourselves as subjects of desire and not as agents of pleasure?

Why does our theory of sex, sexuality, existence, our theory of what it is to be human, the problem of anthropology and philosophical anthropology, deal with the problem of desire, the nature of male and female desire, whereas the problem of pleasure only occupies the smallest part in our theorization, reflection, and ethics? That's the problem I wanted to analyze. I think this slow movement from the conception of mastery [of the self] as the main problem in ethics in the fourth century [BC] to the deciphering of the self in early Christianity is the movement which sees the problem of desire become prevalent. In deciphering the self, the problem is, What is my desire? Do I desire? What is the orientation of my desire? and so on. The hermeneutics of the self, the rise of the hermeneutics of the self, and the prevalence of desire as the main feature of the human, not just of human sexuality, but of the entire human being and existence, is really important, I think. For the Greeks of the fourth century BC, however, the problem was the mastery of oneself which entails the limitation of pleasure. The limitation of pleasure and the deciphering of desire, I think, are two different things, not just two kinds of theories of ethics, but two kinds of relationship to oneself.

We're very interested in knowing ourselves, in figuring out what would be best for ourselves, and so we're very willing to talk to psychoanalysts and confess certain things about ourselves. Those confessions then become material for social theory or psychological theory, which in turn may be used to determine how to take care of people better, how to govern people better so you can get what you want out of them better. Could we say that through the hermeneutics of the self the culture of the self provides a foothold for disciplinary mechanisms in society?

Yes of course, but it depends on the way you do this deciphering of the self. For instance, when this deciphering of the self takes the shape of Christian or Catholic penance, yes, of course the disciplinary effects are very explicit and strong. With psychoanalytical techniques, in psychoanalytical practice, I think the disciplinary effects—and I would like to be prudent—the disciplinary effects are not so evident. I am not saying they don't exist, but they are not as evident as they are in [Catholic penance.]

Could your work on sexuality be used in the study of the past and of women in, say, ancient Greece? I know you're not trying to find a golden age—but it probably would look even drearier than today. Would you envisage undertaking this kind of study?

This is a very important question. First of all, you are quite right, the Greek period was not a golden age for sex at all, even for gay people—if you can use this category for Greek society, which I doubt considerably—but, anyway, it was hard for everybody. The second point I wanted to emphasize is that in this study on the history of sexuality, what I want to do is not the history of behavior, patterns of behavior, or the rules for behavior. It's not a social history of sexual behavior. It's a history of the way our civilization has integrated the problem of sex into the problem of truth or how the problem of truth and the problem of sex have been linked.[96] This leads to psychoanalysis of course, but it also leads to the problem of Christianity which considers the sin of the flesh to be the most significant sin you could commit, and that the true purity of your soul is linked to your obscure sexual desires, to *concupiscence*.[97] That's my problem, not one located in social history, but one located in thought: sex as thought in its relation to truth and to individual truth. In this history, it's a fact that males have played the main role, and only males, since the theory of sex, the rules for techniques of the self, for sexual behavior, and so on, have been imposed by males, by a male society and a male civilization. So, I think this history of the link between truth and sex needs to be done from the male point of view. But of course, and I think this needs to be done, you could also look at the effects of this on the sexual experience, the experience of pleasure, on women's experience of the self, but this of course, would be something else and quite different.

You don't try and refute the theories you analyze, and you don't even consider their truth value. Given the fact that you claim not to be a structuralist, that you claim not to be providing a deeper meaning or conducting a hermeneutics and that you are not appealing to a totality, why should we believe you?

Michel Foucault: There is no reason to.

DISCUSSION WITH
THE DEPARTMENT OF FRENCH

MICHEL FOUCAULT: OK, I'll try and answer your questions. In theory, I think the plan was to use French. But if there are any problems, and if you're happy to listen to my bad English, which is even worse than my French, I'll try and answer in English, if that works better for some of you.[98]

AUDIENCE: *I've been told that you've been asked several times about the difference between your conception of the culture of the self and our Californian vision of hedonism. But no one has been able to explain to me what your answer was.*

That just goes to show that it was a good question and a poor answer. I'll try and improve the answer.

What interests me in Greco-Roman culture—that is, in the Hellenistic culture that began to develop from the third century BC until the second to third century AD—is a phenomenon for which the Greeks had a very specific word, one you find constantly in the texts. This word is *epimeleia heautou*—that is, to take care of oneself, to be concerned with oneself. *Epimeleia* isn't simply a matter of being interested in yourself, it's not just a tendency to self-devotion. *Epimeleia* is a very powerful word in Greek that means "to work on," "to be concerned with." For example, Xenophon used the word *epimeleia* to describe managing an agricultural estate. The word *epimeleia* was also used to refer to the responsibilities of a monarch or a chief and the work he needed to do in relation to his fellow citizens. What a doctor did in caring for a patient was also *epimeleia*. So it's a word that has a very powerful meaning, designating a form of work, an activity—a technique, in short. It's much more a technique of the self, or a work by the self on the self than a simple attention to yourself or [a simple] self-interest. That's the first thing.

The second thing that interests me in this notion, in this practice of the self, is that we can see the birth and development of a certain number of ascetic themes ordinarily attributed to Christianity here. Christianity is credited with having replaced an extremely tolerant Greco-Roman way of life and ethics with a way of life that was, in contrast, austere and characterized by a whole series of renunciations, bans, and prohibitions. But actually, what you begin to realize is that antiquity and ancient morality tied a whole series of austerities, particularly sexual austerities, to this work on the self, to this activity of the self on the self that, basically, Christianity went ahead and borrowed directly. So instead of a grand moral rupture between a pagan and tolerant antiquity and an austere Christianity we should see these practices of the self as slowly giving birth to an austere ethics and a severe and rigorous way of life. That's the second thing that interests me.

The third thing is that this work on the self, with all its austere life consequences, was not imposed on individuals either by civil law or by religious obligation—it was a life choice.

People chose and made their own decisions to care for themselves; it was a sort of life choice and lifestyle they imposed on
themselves. One might ask why they imposed this on themselves. It was not to save their soul and attain eternal life after
death—they didn't believe in this. They did it simply to make
their life into a work of art; they chose this mode of life to create an aesthetics of existence. So, there is this very important
idea, I think, that the principal work of art that needed work,
the principal domain to which aesthetic values and techniques
needed to be applied was yourself, your life, and your existence.[99] This idea has actually been around for quite a long
time in our societies but in slightly attenuated forms. We come
across this idea in the Renaissance and also very strongly in
nineteenth century dandyism—but these were simply epi-
sodes, if you like. Something was missing.

Finally, as a result of all of this, the self you are working on
and trying to elaborate in accordance with aesthetic values is
not something that needs to be discovered after being hidden,
alienated, or disfigured by something else. The self is a work
of art. It's a work of art which, in a way, is right in front of you
needing work. You can only reach who you are at the end of
your life, at the moment of your death. So, there's a very interesting premium placed on old age, your last moments, and
your death in these approaches. Just before you're about to
die or when you're old enough to be close to death, your goal
is to have been able to sculpt a whole life and organize it as a
work of art that will remain immortalized in memory through
its very brilliance. It's at this point that you've truly created
yourself. Hence, I think, the equally important idea of the self
being a creation, you create yourself, you put your own self
together.

You can see a certain number of themes here. I'm not saying

you can reuse these as is, but they do indicate the existence in that culture to which we owe a certain number of our most constant moral elements, of a practice of the self, a conception of the self that's very different from what is currently presented to us as being characteristic of the cult of the self. In the latter, you discover your true self, freeing it from anything that might obscure or alienate it, you decipher its truth through various kinds of psychological and psychoanalytic sciences that have the capacity to tell you what you truly desire. So, not only do I not identify this ancient culture of the self with what you might call the Californian cult of the self, I'd go so far as to say that they are in fact completely opposed. What happened in between was quite precisely a kind of complete reversal of the culture of the self which, I think, took place through Christianity. Christianity replaced the idea of a self you had to create as a work of art through your own efforts in life with the idea of a self you had to renounce, since clinging to yourself was to oppose the will of God. It was a self that had to be both renounced and deciphered because it was there that the primary elements of concupiscence, desire, the flesh, and so on came to be lodged and rooted. Once the self became something to be renounced rather than created, no longer a work of art to be measured against aesthetic values but something to be deciphered like an obscure text, it is here, I think, that we see a reversal of the experience of self in a way that's quite characteristic of Christianity.[100] So the opposition between paganism and Christianity is not between tolerance and austerity but between a form of austerity that is linked to an aesthetics of the culture of the self and other forms of austerity that are linked to the necessity of renouncing yourself and deciphering your true self.

I might have misunderstood, but at one point, like Lacan, you

said that the ego [moi] *is something that is created, and I think*
you might have also said that the ego is something that's already
in place.

Listen, I didn't use the word "ego" [*moi*]. The words I use
are "individual," "subject," "self," and "relation to the self." In
any case, I wouldn't be able to give a precise meaning to the
ego. Also, I'm not sure that Lacan said that the ego was a creation.

I'm not sure either.

Well, let's agree on our mutual uncertainty! And let's leave
aside the hypothesis of Lacan cobbling together the ego on
the fly.

I'd like to ask you two questions about the relationship between
writing and the culture of the self. How does writing contribute to
the development of the culture of the self? Also, how has this devel-
opment taken on an aesthetic dimension through writing?

These are two very good questions. The first is on the relationship between writing and the problem of the culture of
the self. You are asking if there was something in writing that
could be linked in with and allow the culture of the self to
develop in a particular way.

I can't answer you there. But because it's an important and
difficult question, I'd like to go ahead and draw attention first
to a certain number of empirical elements that are very often
neglected when we raise this problem of writing. This is the
famous problem of the *hupomnēmata*.[101] Indeed, when we see
a certain critique of the *hupomnēmata* in the famous text of the
Phaedrus,[102] we tend not to give this word *hupomnēmata* any
meaning beyond the elements that might serve as a material
aid to memory, specifically writing.

Now, in fact, *hupomnēmata* has a very precise meaning, it
is a very precise object. What are *hupomnēmata*? This word

means a notebook. And it was exactly this kind of notebook that was starting to spread and become a habit in classical Athens at the time. It was both a political and an administrative instrument, with, for example, taxes on individual commercial transactions and charges being noted down in *hupomnēmata*. Thus it was an instrument of political administration. For the owners of agricultural and commercial private enterprises, the *hupomnēmata* were also a means of recording activities that had been completed or needed to be done. And then, finally, it was an instrument for managing one's personal life, a means of keeping a record of completed tasks and especially what needed to be done. It allowed people to recall at the start of the day what needed to be done during the day. The introduction of *hupomnēmata*, not simply as a general material aid to memory, but as the material instruments I have just mentioned was just as disruptive as the introduction of computers has been today in everyday life. But this comparison is probably facile and not very interesting. So this was the technical and material framework, if you like, that surrounded this question of the *hupomnēmata*. The first example, that I know of at least—there might be others—of these *hupomnēmata* is in Xenophon's *Memorabilia* when, right at the end, he mentions Socrates giving advice to his disciples.[103] Socrates gives them advice on health: how to maintain good health and what diet to follow. Here we see the influence of hippocratism and those dietary practices that derive both from Pythagoreanism and medicine. It is quite remarkable that in the *Memorabilia* Socrates instructs his disciples to note down in *hupomnēmata* what they are eating, how they react to what they are eating, and also what diet they are following. So here we have the *hupomnēmata*.

Second, now for another set of problems. This is the problem that's raised, or the problems that are raised by the text of the *Phaedrus* and its famous critique of writing, insofar as writing is opposed to the culture of memory. Now if you read the *Phaedrus*, you can see that these remarks are fleeting in comparison with another more fundamental idea that runs through the entire text right to the end—namely, that it's not important whether a discourse is written or oral; the problem is knowing whether this discourse is indexed to the truth or not. And you realize that for Plato at that time the problem of writing versus the oral was completely secondary to this fundamental question.

Third, what I would like to say is this. What seems quite remarkable to me about this problem of the culture of the self and techniques of the self, was that these new instruments, the instruments of memorization through writing, the *hupomnēmata*, seemed to have been used immediately in establishing a permanent relation to the self. It's certainly true that the aspects of political administration and property management [were of great importance]* in this management of the self and in this idea that you must manage yourself, just as a governor manages the governed, a business manager manages his business, and a household head manages his household. But I think there was also something very important here in terms of the development of an idea that we see across the centuries virtually right up until Christianity, and that's the theme that virtue essentially consists in governing oneself perfectly, that is, in exercising a mastery over oneself as exacting as a sovereignty against which there can be no revolt. So, if you like, the point where I think you can see the question of the *hupomnēmata* and the question of the culture of the self come into

---

* Conjecture; inaudible passage.

play in quite a remarkable way, is this point where the culture of the self set the goal of perfect self government, a kind of permanent political relationship between self and self. Thus we have to build a politics of ourselves.[104] And this politics of ourselves is carried out in the sense that we materially put together *hupomnēmata*, just as governments and business owners are obliged to keep records. This is how writing appears to me to be related to the problem of the culture of the self.

What I've outlined here is hardly an overview or a program—it's more a series of questions, but what needs to be studied are the different modes of writing we see developing at the time. It seems to me that there are two main modes of self-writing, or writing that makes the culture of the self possible.[105] One of these is the much vaunted *hupomnēmata* as notebooks we keep on ourselves, and which appear to be completely different from what we find later in Christianity and even more so from what we find in the sixteenth century, that is the journals where you talk about yourself, your own experiences, your everyday life, and so on. I think the *hupomnēmata* always continued to be collections of precepts, collections of things you needed to know or do. You noted your readings, conversations you had heard, the master's lessons and notes for what could serve as a framework, as it were, of a permanent set of rules for life in the *hupomnēmata*. In these notebooks you recorded the permanent set of rules that were to be internalized by the permanent rereading of the *hupomnēmata*.

On the other hand, the account of yourself, the texts where you discussed what you did during the day, your impressions and encounters with others, all of this belongs to the dimension that includes the account or description of yourself. It's no longer a matter of prescriptions for oneself, but of self-description. You don't find this in the *hupomnēmata*, you find this in correspondence, in letters; that is when someone else is present. Now, it seems the evolution of the epistolary genre was very noticeable over a short period of time—for example, from Cicero to Seneca. When Cicero writes to his friends, it's to say, "You know, Mark Anthony causes me these kinds of worries, I have this kind of problem and so on." These are always business letters, political letters. Cicero practically never talks about himself, except to mention that he has health problems or that he made such and such a trip and so on. On the other hand, you find a completely different self-description in Seneca. For example you find in his letters—I think it's letter 55—a description of a walk around his property, where he walked on the sand, saw the sea on one side and on the other, the property of one of his old friends now dead, and so on.[106] And then he records his impressions, his physical impressions, the way he breathed in the air, the way his asthmatic shortness of breath was soothed by the sea air, the memories that came to him when he noticed the villa of his now deceased friend and so on. You have a real self-description that seems to be absolutely new, at least if you compare it to Cicero. There is fifty years difference here.[107] Here you have a description, a description that was meant for others. I think the day the personal notebook, the *hupomnēmata*, became something other than a reminder of what to do or what needed to be remembered to conduct oneself properly, and when the *hupomnēmata*, the personal notebook, became the description of self, that is the day you have Saint Athanasius's account of Saint Anthony. In this account he says that Saint Anthony had a notebook with him in which he wrote down all the temptations he suffered during the night, the demonic visions, everything suggested by Satan to make him fall.[108] There you have the beginnings of the narrative of the self.

So, if you like, there is obviously a gigantic evolution between the *hupomnēmata* Xenophon mentions, where it was
just a matter of reminding oneself of the elements of the
regimen and the description of the nocturnal temptations
of Saint Anthony. But you still have a transition between the
two and that is in the description of dreams. It seems that very
early on you were expected to describe your own dreams in
the *hupomnēmata*, and you have testimonies to this. Artemidorus's account is not clear, but it is implicit.[109] In any case,
you have Synesius's very clear testimony.[110] Synesius was a
pagan who converted to Christianity at the beginning of the
fourth century, I think, and he seems to link this to a tradition.
I don't remember the exact details, but in any case he wasn't
really any earlier than Saint Anthony,[111] so you can't make the
link through him. But Synesius does mention what seems to
have been a very common practice at the time—namely, that
of course you needed to know, note down, and interpret your
dreams so as to know what events to expect or watch out for.
You had to have a notebook next to you at night where you
wrote down your dreams so you could either interpret them
yourself the next morning or show them to someone who
could interpret them for you. Right there, through this description of the night, it seems an important step was taken
toward intimate self-description in notebooks.

That's what I wanted to say about writing. That's all I know
for the moment and I am summarizing what I am able to say
at this point. To put it simply, it's true that problems of the
rhetorical structure of discourse self-referenced to the person
writing were very important and that this whole problem of
the institutionalization of self-writing within a practice of the
self, a culture of oneself, is interesting, But I'm interested in
this because I don't think you can understand Montaigne's

Essays for example, if you don't keep in mind this gigantic culture and practice of the self through writing that was already almost two thousand years old when Montaigne was writing.

If I've understood it correctly from what you've just said, the hupomnēmata *that prescribed what had to be done introduced elements that were more difficult to control through writing, such as dreams and sensations.*

I think that through this evolution of the practice of writing you see . . . in a way, this constitutes a parser of the modifications of the relationships that you can have with yourself. Basically, when I am talking about the *hupomnēmata* as prescriptions, what am I referring to? I am referring to that notion that is so important in Greece and Greek culture—namely, the notion of *gnōmē*; *gnōmē* which is, as you know, usually a brief formula, often formulated by a poet, a formula that speaks the truth, the essential and fundamental truth that needs to be remembered. At the same time, it is piece of advice, an opinion, a life rule. *Gnōmē* is both truth and rule, truth and norm.[112] And that is basically what *hupomnēmata* are. One of the first things you write in the *hupomnēmata* is some aphorism or other or a *gnōmē* that might have been taken from a poet—maybe Pindar or Hesiod—whatever. You note these down and reread them from time to time to really get them into your head. Much later we find a whole heap of traces of all these practices in Marcus Aurelius. But what interests me is the transition from *hupomnēmata* as a recording of life rules to be remembered to the progressive description of oneself that becomes clear, and not just clear but obligatory in Saint Anthony, using dream journaling as an intermediary as Athanasius describes. Recording dreams was the precise transition point, as the dream is both something that happened to you, and something you are obliged to recount. You recount your dream so you know what to do and what measures you need to take, given the dream might announce a particular event, for example your marriage, the death of your parents, or a future shipwreck, and so on. From there, you can work out what to do. So the account of a dream is an account of the self, a description and diagnosis of what you need to do, a prescription.

Would the transition from gnōmē *to narrative have had aesthetic consequences for self-writing?*

Yes, sorry, I didn't answer you on the aesthetic problem, which was your second question—I am a bit less sure on this point. I don't have the impression that there ever was a clear explanation of the need to give an aesthetic form to this self-narrative until a lot later. There are Seneca's letters, which are really very artificial, to the extent that it's hard to know how far they really were effectively an exchange with Lucilius, rather than a way they both used to create a work of art together. Thus, we can consider these descriptive letters of Seneca's, in particular the very elegant one I'm referring to,[113] to have been deliberately designed to be beautiful. They follow obvious aesthetic criteria. But what's striking is that in all the theories, [or rather] the few elements of theory relating to epistolary literature we find in antiquity, and in particular in the famous text by Demetrius I referred to earlier which came late in the piece,[114] you see, the letter was always seen to constitute and pertain to the most basic level of rhetoric. You must really open your heart and just speak without artifice— well actually, not without too much artifice . . . You have an interesting letter from Seneca responding to Lucilius saying, "You are asking me to embellish my letters, that you are finding them too simple, but at the end of the day a letter is meant to be simple."[115] So there was a tension between the aesthetic value of the letter and its simplicity. But still, generally by and large letters were designed to be simple and I don't think the aesthetic of self-narrative, the voluntary aesthetic was ever reflected in antiquity.

I am intrigued by what you have to say about the letter. As you know, writing was criticized for being a poor tool as it compromised memory and, if you wrote, you no longer needed to exercise your memory. Was the letter devalued as well?

Yes, but you know this devaluation of writing on the pretext that it might hinder memory, was very fleeting and very precarious, and once again this is something you find in the text of the *Phaedrus*. There's a passage that says it clearly: it doesn't matter whether a discourse is written or oral, the problem is how to determine whether the discourse is true.[116] So I don't think we should overestimate this problem of the rejection of writing too much. It was probably just one of those knee-jerk reactions like the ones that currently make us reject home computers on the pretext that they they have meant beautiful family share certificates being torn up.[117] It's a crisis that is skin deep. What seems more important to me is the Platonic assertion that written or oral, a discourse must be true. That's where the real difference lies.

Do you make a distinction between the care of the self and self-knowledge? Or are they the same thing?

No. Obviously, they're closely linked, but they are very different. And there too, I believe that we have a phenomenon similar to the one I was trying to explain when I mentioned this long slide, this deviation from the principle of *gnōmē* to the principle of the description of self. We must remember first in relation to the principle that we must know ourselves, that for the whole time, right from the beginning, even in Plato, even in Xenophon, when the Socratic formulation was used, it was always linked to the another principle, namely "taking care of yourself," *epimeleia heautou*, "working on yourself." The relationship between these two precepts was always complex and merits analyis.[118] In general, the formulation is as follows (in any case it's the one found in the *Alcibiades*): it's necessary to take care of yourself, because if you don't take care of yourself, you can't perform the governing role that you wish to perform in society. This is what Socrates said to Alcibiades. Alcibiades then asked but what do you do to take care of yourself? Well, says Plato, you first need to know what "to take care of" means and then what "self" means.[119] This is how he introduces the necessity of knowing yourself, as implied by the more general and more fundamental principle of caring for oneself.[120] We could find different texts that accentuate the *gnōthi seauton* more than the *epimeleia heautou*, but it doesn't matter, let's just say you have this constant connection in Plato.

Now, if you take the theme of "knowing yourself," a theme that is striking in Socratic texts and the Socratic tradition— namely, in Xenophon and Plato—you see that this knowledge of self never takes shape except through something like the discovery of what the soul itself is, the *psuchē*, as an immaterial, immortal and pure principle. That is, it's the knowledge of the soul's mode of being that makes up the fundamental element of the *gnōthi seauton*. This ontological knowledge of the self as a soul is conducted, at least in certain texts and in particular in the *Alcibiades*, in the form of contemplation, of the contemplation of the soul by it itself, using the famous metaphor of the eye: how can the eye see itself? The answer is apparently very simple but is in fact very complicated. Plato doesn't say that all one has to do is look in a mirror. Instead the eye must look into another eye—that is, into itself, but into itself in the form of the eye of the other, and further into the pupil of the eye of the other. The eye will see itself since the pupil serves as a mirror. In the same way the soul will see itself and recognize itself as a divine element in contemplating itself in another soul, or in the divine element of that soul which is like the pupil of that other soul.[121]

Let's leave aside this problem of contemplation in its strict sense. Anyway, this idea that you need to know yourself, either in general so as to gain ontological knowledge of the soul's mode of being, or effectively, as a specific act of consultation is entirely independent of what you might call a exercise of self on the self. When it comes to grasping your soul's mode of being, you don't need to ask yourself what you've done, what you're thinking about, what the movement of your ideas is, your representations and what you're attached to, which is of course absolutely [perceptible],* visible, and concrete, as it were. What is striking is that, in the culture of self that developed from the third century, and particularly in the wake of the Stoic influence . . . I am saying "particularly in the wake of Stoic influence" because the Epicureans left very little behind about these practices of self-examination, apart from a few things by Philodemus, but not much. We just know that in Epicurean groups you had to examine yourself every day.[122] And then they examined each other, and it seems that there were group sessions where people talked about the self and where the others helped you to examine yourself. But we only know this through Philodemus's very fragmentary and somewhat cryptic texts.[123] On the other hand, the Stoic literature is much richer. There we see that the need to know oneself had a very different style from the Socratic literature of Xenophon or Plato. In a certain type of Stoicism, in particular in late Stoicism, like Epictetus, you'll find very explicit and very

* Conjecture; inaudible word.

strong references to Socrates, to the *gnōthi seauton* and so on. But this *gnōthi seauton* has a [different] meaning, it took shape in a completely different way in the texts of late Stoicism. For a start, it takes the form of absolutely regular exercises, and in particular in the famous vesperal examination, the evening examination, where you go through your day and call to mind what you have done.[124] You find this theme which is of Pythagorean origin in the Stoics. All the texts are in agreement on this. But Plato, influenced and impressed by Pythagoreanism as he was, never ever speaks about the examination of conscience. Taking hold of one's soul and contemplating it in its own being, doesn't involve going through the exercise of asking "what good have I done and what harm have I done?" before going to bed in the evening. You find exercises like this in the Stoics. Epictetus also developed a kind of ambulatory self-examination that involved paying attention to different objects you came across while walking and asking yourself whether you were attached to them or not and whether you felt independent of desire for them or not.[125] You come across a consular personage: are you impressed by his pomp and do you want to become a consul? You meet a pretty woman or an atractive boy: do you want to go to bed with him or her? It's that kind of thing. Epictetus says you must do this every morning. You go out and then ... You also find another form of very interesting self-examination in Marcus Aurelius. Marcus Aurelius says—and this is very interesting because it is linked to the theme of *hupomnēmata* and apparently in opposition to it ... Marcus Aurelius says that from time to time, we must close all the books, no longer bring anything to mind and engage in *anakhōrēsis eis heauton, anachoresis* within oneself, a retreat within oneself. Then you try to go over the principles of conduct that you need to hold to, those you remember and realize are always there in a very present and very active form ready to bring into action if needed.[126] This reactivation of the principles of conduct in that virtual book which is yourself and in the memory of which the rules of behavior are written constitutes another form of self-examination.

I'm emphasizing this for two reasons. First, you find none of this in the strictly Socratic and Platonic tradition. Neoplatonism is much more interested in problems of purification than problems of examination. Second, you can see that these self-examinations are different from those you go on to find in Christianity. In Christianity it's a matter of knowing through self-examination whether there remains any specific trace of impurity, concupiscence, or any specific element of the flesh that might lead you into a specific [sin].* What is at stake in the self-examinations in Stoic literature is essentially knowing whether you have a good grasp of the baggage of the rules of conduct you need for everyday life. If you go over your day, it's to know where you have made mistakes and then through remembering where you've made mistakes, you reactivate the rules of conduct you should have applied and didn't. This is much more than an exercise in memorization with the aim of blaming oneself, it's about using the errors, *hamartēmata*,[127] of the day to remind oneself of the rules. It's about renewing the code, much more than a deepening of guilt. In a similar fashion, the exercises of self-examination while walking, ascertaining whether you are attached to this or that, don't involve discovering some deep and hidden desire, but in knowing to what extent you are free in relation to everything that can lead you astray. It's a test of your current freedom, of self-control—not the discovery of secret misdoing.[128] So, you see, this is a

---

* Conjecture; inaudible word.

whole other style of relationship to the self, which seems at the same time to be both very different from Platonic contemplation, and very different from what will come to be the Christian examination of conscience.

What is the place of techniques of the self from antiquity in the renewal of the culture of the self in the sixteenth century?

I am not going to put forward a hypothesis on this front. I don't know whether there have been any precise or reasonably succinct studies of these practices of self-examination or the self in the sixteenth century. Very approximately, it would seem obvious that from the end of the fifteenth century in the religious crisis and the great rejection you see of the practices of the Catholic pastoral, the type of confession, of priests and the exercise of institutional authority over people, in this rejection, I think a form of relationship with the self and search for a new way of relating to the self was developing. Second, it appears to me that the reactivation of a number of ancient and Stoic themes and practices in this search are [quite visible].* I even think that the notion of the essay in Montaigne is quite close to themes we find in the Stoics. I am speaking of the essay understood in the strict sense of the word—namely, a test, we measure ourselves against what we need to and we see whether and how far we can go and so on, a notion which is a kind of test of oneself. For the Stoics, self-examination was undertaken less as an attempt to discover a form hidden deep within oneself, a truth hidden deep inside, than an attempt to know and challenge what we know and don't know. It was a test of what we can do and what we can't, a test of the freedom we have and of how far we are dependent, the dependencies to which we are still attached.[129] Testing the self as well as de-

---

* Conjecture; inaudible passage.

ciphering the self seem pretty evident to me in Montaigne, but
I may be wrong.

Couldn't we see in the Spiritual Exercises *of Loyola, in a sense,*
the opposite of the renaissance of these ancient practices of self?

Yes, they are both the opposite and then . . . What's very
striking in Loyola's *Exercises* and all these spiritual exercises,[130]
is not so much the way individuals were obliged to pay attention to themselves to decipher a secret truth but rather the
provision of a kind of permanent instrument, a permanent
framework, that allowed individuals to be actively engaged
with themselves and others throughout the entire day. I am
fully aware there are moments in Loyola when you have to
look within and discern, but these are just high points, passing
moments. [In] this great framing of life as exercise, which is
so remarkable in all these spiritual exercises from Loyola onwards, what is striking, on the contrary, is the fact that something is needed at every moment. You need to direct your
thinking in a specific way and secure your own independence,
or rather your own dependence in relation to God. And then
you could . . . And this might be a bit arbitrary, because it's
likely that the texts don't address this directly, but I remember finding in a seventeenth century text—not a Jesuit text,
it was a text, I believe, for French seminaries, but anyway it
doesn't matter—a formula for walking that is reminiscent of
Epictetus. In this text every time the individual, the young
seminarist, sees something while out walking, he must do
an exercise that allows him to discover how this thing shows
his dependence on God. This enables him to make an act of
thanks for the divine goodness that allows him to decipher
the presence of divine providence. Once again, it's likely that
these two texts don't correspond with each other, as although
the Epictetus's *Manual* was very well known, the *Discourses*

less so. There's not really any reason that this text . . . But in fact, they do correspond with each other to the extent that in Epictetus, the individual confirms his own sovereignty over himself and shows that he doesn't depend on any of the things he sees during the walk. In the other case, the seminarist goes for a walk and every time he sees something, he says, "Oh, how great is the goodness of God, He who made this and who holds everything in his power, myself in particular. I renounce my own will and accept the will of God." Two exercises in walking meditation.

It's like a kind of rosary . . .

Yes, that's it, absolutely. But then, I think all the literature that's about the self strictly speaking—personal accounts, personal diaries, and so on—can only be understood if it is placed within the very general and very rich context of those practices of the self which are now two and a half thousand years old. Two and a half millennia of people writing about themselves, but not in the same way. This is something that's extremely important in our culture. In all of this, you can really see that writing and having a relation to yourself are two very different things. I have the impression, but I may be wrong, that there is a certain tendency to present the relationship between writing and everyday life as a phenomenon peculiar to European modernity. But I'd say its origins are not just modern, that this was in fact one of the first uses of writing.

Can we escape from this cycle of writing about yourself?

I think that taking care of yourself is something that is indeed—I dare not say a cultural invariant—as there is nothing except variation in all of this. For example, historians have always attached great importance to the, let's say, objective techniques that the individual exercises in relation to objects, to the things he or she creates and so on. There has also been a lot of study, even if it has been insufficient, I think, of what we might call the technology of others—that is, the way in which we manage others, through institutions, politics, through various rules and disciplinary constraints and so on. Then there is also the problem of the techniques of the self. We find these techniques of self in all cultures, I think, but just in extremely different forms. Just as we need to study, compare, and differentiate techniques of the production of objects across civilizations as well as techniques relating to the management of people and their direction and government, we also need to raise the problem of techniques of the self.[131] And techniques of the self change. Obviously, two things make the analysis of these techniques of the self difficult. First, techniques of the self obviously don't require the same material underpinnings as the production of objects, so they are often invisible. Second, they are frequently closely linked to the techniques of the direction of others. For example, if we take the institution of education: in educating, we manage others [in the first instance], and then we teach them to manage themselves. So, we have a technique of the self which would appear to be completely linked to a technique of others. Hence, for these two reasons it is more difficult to analyze techniques of the self: they are more obscure than the big visible material techniques—for example, love, the production of [objects].* But it is nonetheless [something that is still visible],† whether in religious or parareligious systems, or assimilated into religious systems like Buddhism (strictly speaking Buddhism is still essentially a technique of the self, much more than a religion and much more than a moral system.)[132] In any so-

* Conjecture; inaudible passage.
† Conjecture; inaudible passage.

called primitive society, I think, you will also find elements of techniques of the self.

Do you think that ancient society was a society based on shame, with shame playing a fundamental role?[133]

No, I don't think so. I was pleased to see a very good book by MacMullen on *Roman Social Relations*,[134] where he takes that up—the society of shame or the society of guilt. Mac-Mullen responds clearly by saying, "Civilization of shame? I can't see it. What I see among the Romans, is rather a civilization of glory, a *pride society* and not a *guilt society*." He stresses the importance of status, bearing, and how to walk. This regulation of movement and physical attitude was incredibly important for the Romans. It was a technique of the self which was immediately directed toward others, as it was a question of ensuring status, precedence, and consequently an influence over others. This clearly doesn't derive from a *shame society* but from a *pride society*.

The ancient techniques of self-cultivation seem to have been completely obscured by Christianity and by Western philosophy, where it's no longer a question of cultivating a self but of establishing an ego. But do you detect traces of something in the following eras that might be similar to the ancient idea of a relationship with oneself, traces of this culture of the self?

That's a good question. First, I don't believe that this culture of self was obscured or disappeared. You can find many elements that were simply integrated, displaced, and reused in Christianity. And many of the elements of what is described as Christian asceticism come from this culture of self. Second, when the culture of the self was taken up by Christianity, it was, in a way, brought under the purview of the exercise of a pastoral power insofar as *the epimeleia heautou* essentially became *epimeleia tōn allōn*, the care of others the pastor must engage in. I think the culture of self lost a large part of its autonomy once everyone's salvation started to pass, at least in part, through a pastoral institution whose object was the care of souls. This doesn't mean it disappeared. It was integrated and lost part of its autonomy.

On the other hand, what's interesting is that during the Renaissance you see a whole series of religious groups working against the effects of power generated by these pastoral institutions. These groups whose existence was already evident in the Middle Ages, resisted this pastoral power claiming they could achieve salvation through their own efforts, either as individuals on their own or as groups acting independently of the ecclesiastical institution and ecclesiastical pastorate.[135] So up to a certain point, there was a rebirth, not of the culture of the self, which hadn't disappeared, but a rebirth of its autonomy, a reappearance of more autonomous forms. You can also see this in the Renaissance—and I refer you to Burckhardt's text here,[136] which should perhaps be reread to a degree from this perspective—in particular the well-known and famous chapter on the aesthetics of existence with the hero as his own work of art. The idea that that you needed to turn life and your own life into a work of art reappeared at that time and was an idea that was probably quite foreign to the Middle Ages. The history is very complex, if you like. In the dandyism of the nineteenth century, you obviously also had a . . .

I was wondering if you were going to talk about Nietzsche.

No, because—and pardon the colloquial expression—I think he completely had the wrong end of the stick when it came to asceticism—more specifically Christian asceticism. Also, even if the idea of a Nietzschean genealogy can and should be invoked to analyze this genre, everything he had to say about asceticism and Christian asceticism appears to fall short when it comes to [what we know about pagan morals.*] I don't think you can reinterpret or reread Nietzsche in any way as a reappearance or a reactivation of the theme of the culture of the self. But maybe I'm wrong. It might be worth reconsidering . . .

But you know, all [this]. I thought about it when I needed to take a look at the ancient texts and wanted to do some genealogy of sexual prohibitions in our societies. I realized that it was not a problem to do with the code at all, that is a problem of injunction-prohibition—the real problem in the history of morality was the history of these practices of self. What is forbidden has always been the same. And we are societies who have invented very little in the order of prohibitions and the same goes for the order of desire—God knows how little we've invented in the order of desire! Equally, very little has been created in the order of the prohibition of pleasures. It's always the same thing that's prohibited. So that's not what's interesting. On the other hand, what is interesting in the history of morality is this technology of self which has continued to change, to enrich, and amplify itself and commit to [new]† forms.[137] So this led me to look at all of this. It's really obvious in antiquity, a period of history that saw a real development of the technique of the self and presented philosophy as a technique of the self. The idea of a philosophy as a general system of the world or as the foundation of science was completely foreign, or in any case relatively rare in ancient philosophy, even if there were some major and important formulations

---

* Conjecture; inaudible passage.
† Conjecture; inaudible passage.

which we cling onto now. But let's just say, that in its daily development, day by day, ancient philosophy was a practice of
the self. If you needed to know about the course of the stars or
whether atoms existed or not, it was so as to be able to medi-
tate on oneself, it was an exercise.[138] We truly have a culture of
self which developed on its own terms during this period, with
its own autonomy and institutions, with teachers and teachers
of the self. There were people you went to consult, who you
asked about how to behave, what was good, what wasn't good
and so on. This was a golden age.

*I was struck by the break between Montaigne and Descartes. In
Montaigne you see the presence of techniques of the self, whereas
with Descartes, you see the* mise en abyme *and even the subver-
sion of these techniques. How might the elaboration of the subject
have interrupted, subverted, or even hijacked these techniques of
the self?*

What's happening here is very interesting. Let's start by
saying that the relationship between Montaigne, Pascal, and
Descartes could basically be reread in the light of this very interesting question. Pascal, too, can be seen not just as a critic
of Montaigne but as someone who belongs to a tradition, or
who has deliberately placed himself in a tradition, in which the
practices of self and asceticism are of a completely different
order from Montaigne's practices of the self. Second, we must
not forget, of course, that Descartes wrote the *Meditations*—
and meditation is a practice of the self. In his extraordinary
text, Descartes, very explicitly adopted the model of a process
of meditation, of an Ignatian daily exercise repeated several
times a day. I think it was precisely the torsion you refer to that
allowed him to substitute a founding subject of practices of
knowledge for a subject constructed through practices of the
self. The "Cartesian moment" involved going from a subject

produced by a practice of the self to a subject as founder of a practice of knowledge.[139] But once again, like Montaigne and Pascal, this was against the background of those broad confrontations around the technologies of the self, which were extremely important culturally in the sixteenth and seventeenth centuries.

So, in this instance, I think that what happened at the time, was actually quite fundamental and went roughly something like this. Basically, from Greek philosophy onwards, even if it's true that Greek philosophy founded modern scientific rationality, we always had the idea a subject could not have access to the truth without a certain work on the self, enabling that subject to know the truth. This work involved purification, the conversion of the soul and the self-contemplation of the soul which were Platonic exercises. You also have the Stoic theme of the exercise where the subject ensured its autonomy and independence first, through a fairly complex relationship with knowledge [connaissance] about the world. Knowledge of the world allowed the subject to ensure its independence, and once this independence was assured it could, at that moment, recognize the order of the world for what it was. This question can be found throughout European culture up until the sixteenth century: What work must I do on myself to make me able and worthy of arriving at the truth and for that truth to be given to me? What purification, what exercises, what ascetic practices must I engage in? In other words, truth has a price; you must always pay a price to access truth; there can be no access to the truth without asceticism.[140] Asceticism and knowledge of the truth are always more or less obscurely linked. From this perspective, you can see how alchemical knowledge, which involved both work on oneself and knowledge of the truth with the two linked so closely as to be almost inseparable, could be a normal part of received knowledge.[141] In fact, the "Cartesian moment" had already begun, and you could do the genealogy of this in the sixteenth century. I think Descartes summed it all up when he said that to have access to the truth it was enough to be any subject who could see what is evident. At that point evidence replaced asceticism as the junction point between the relation to oneself and to truth. The relation to the self no longer needed to be ascetic to transform oneself in relation to the truth. It was enough that the relation to the self revealed the obvious truth of what I saw for me to grasp it, and to grasp it definitively. I can therefore be immoral and know the truth.[142] Basically, I think this was an idea that was more or less explicitly, rejected by all of Greek culture. One cannot literally be impure or immoral and know the truth. But with Descartes, it was enough to see the evidence. From that moment, we had a nonascetic subject of knowledge, which allowed the institutionalization of science, and allows completely immoral people to become chairs of scientific departments, something which would not have been possible otherwise . . . Plato couldn't be immoral. I am taking enormous shortcuts in sketching a very long but I think fundamental history.

So, from that moment we have a subject of knowledge, a unique subject of knowledge, which goes on to pose a certain problem for Kant—and I'm answering your question here. The problem concerned the relationship between the moral subject and knowledge and whether it would be completely different or not. There's indecision around this for the whole of the eighteenth century. Kant's solution was to have found the universal subject, which, insofar as it was universal, could be the subject of knowledge [*connaissance*], but it still required a moral attitude, and it was precisely this type of relationship to the self that Kant proposed in *The Critique of Practical Reason*. He postulated that I must recognize myself as a universal subject—that is, I must, in each of my actions, create myself as the universal subject of a universal rule.[143] So, if we haven't solved the problem of the moral subject, at least we are proposing a solution that makes it possible to put the moral subject in a position that is different from the subject of knowledge. The moral subject and the subject of knowledge were no longer directly related, but this solution is very ambiguous. There is the evidence, since any subject can know, and moral action is action which obeys a universal rule. Cartesian evidence and the Kantian universality of moral action seem to respond in two steps, to this problem posed by the great crisis in the culture of the self in the sixteenth century.

What allows the passage from the self to the subject?

The practice of the self, or what I'm calling the practice of the self, is the way in which the individual, in the relation he has to him or herself, constitutes him or herself as a subject. How can I constitute myself as a moral subject and recognize myself as a moral subject? To become a moral subject of my action, what do I do need to do to myself? Do I need to undertake ascetic exercises, or do I just need this Kantian relationship that allows me to discover myself as the subject of an action whose rule must be universal? So, there you have it. You create yourself as a subject in relation to the self, the subject is not a given. It is the relationship to the self that makes up [subjectivity*].[144] In other words, what underpins my discourse is this: It is not enough to say that the subject constituted itself in a symbolic system; the subject constitutes itself through real practices, through practices that can be historically ana-

* Conjecture; inaudible word.

lyzed. There is a technology of the constitution of the subject that runs through symbolic systems and uses them, but the subject is not simply constituted through the play of symbolic systems. We are at the polemical cutting edge [here].*

There's a whole tradition from Plato to Abelard, which sees the eunuch as the perfect philosopher. Abelard wonders, since he has been castrated, whether he is as perfect as Origen, who castrated himself.

You're absolutely right, I hadn't thought of that. The problem of the eunuch was very important when Christian asceticism began: should one go ahead and castrate oneself if effectively it is the purification of the body and the soul that grants access to eternal life? The general answer is along these lines: it is not true purity if you no longer need to purify yourself and maintain a perpetual battle with your own desires. And then there is a whole lot of very amusing literature, which I love, on the impure desires of castrates. If the body of the castrate is no longer capable of impurity, their soul, on the other hand, must be incredibly dark . . .

Are there any other questions? Listen, on the one hand thank you very much for your attention and for your really interesting questions. All I can say is that I apologize: I haven't even presented you with an outline, [but rather with] a kind of draft, [something] along those lines. There seems to be a whole field of work that exists on the borders of a political history and a history of knowledge that would be interesting to study. I started looking at this a bit in antiquity, but I'm sure that in the periods that interest us most, the Middle Ages, the Renaissance, and [the] seventeenth to eighteenth centuries . . . Oh, here you go, there is something that I would be interested

* Conjecture; inaudible passage.

in doing: studying revolutionary movements as ascetic and practical movements of the self.[145] Yes, the revolution in the nineteenth century was like truth was up until the sixteenth century, you couldn't engage in it without being morally pure and giving up a certain number of things. Revolutionary asceticism has been extremely important and its disastrous consequences are still emerging today.

Do you mean that revolution presupposes moral purity?

That's right. There is a very old book in the library here, written in an incomprehensible style, or at least in nineteenth century academic style . . . Worse than ours? Who knows . . . It is by the moralist Martha,[146] who makes interesting connections with movements of moralization. In particular, he makes connections between what was happening in Rome at the beginning of the Empire, what happened during the French Revolution and the examination of conscience. The Revolution's allusions to Rome, you know, were not simply a stylistic flourish of course, and there was a somewhat artificial attempt to reconstruct a mode of the culture of the self, rethinking it in revolutionary terms. I was thinking mainly of the revolutionary movements which developed after 1830 in Europe, particularly among the nihilists—a very interesting ascetic and aesthetic movement.[147] Renunciation of the self and violence against others, all of that happened and it's very interesting. I think a history of revolution could be done, not just as the history of political movements of course, but also as a history of morality, the latter envisaged as a practice of the self, as a set of practices of the self. And the odious moralism of Stalinism will only be the end point of this history of the revolution . . .

Can we see an extension of Greek culture in existentialism, in its concern for self-study and engagement?

Yes, well . . . It's absolutely true that Sartre is a Stoic. If you wanted to investigate what Sartre is closest to, it would quite precisely be a Stoic, a Stoic with some notions on Fichte . . .

But where I would still make a very big distinction, is that Sartre still fundamentally subscribes to the idea of authenticity—and God knows, he is someone who really distrusts psychoanalysis and never really took it on. This authenticity, I think, is very different from what the Stoics understood by living in accordance with nature and what they understood as self-appropriation, very different from this idea of a self created as a work of art. You are right in noticing the similarities; but, you know, these sorts of recurrences can't be used as a critical instrument. We could well argue that Montaigne's work was a series of reactivations of the Epicureans, Stoics, and skeptics. This is true but at the same time it's different. With Sartre . . . it's very interesting—I haven't read what they have just published on morality, his writings on morality.[148] I am not familiar with what he's done. He certainly tried to write on this subject his entire life but never managed to publish this work. He could never quite bring it up to the right level. It's clear that the essential aim of his research wasn't how we can construct a new morality, or a form of ethics . . . It seems to me that he was very close to the Stoics. He was at the same time both aware but also unaware of this proximity and this prevented him from [going through with it].*

* Conjecture; inaudible passage.

NOTES

Introduction

1. Immanuel Kant, "An Answer to the Question: What Is Enlightenment? (1784)," in *Practical Philosophy*, ed. Mary J. Gregor, 11–22, The Cambridge Edition of the Works of Immanuel Kant (Cambridge: Cambridge University Press, 1996).

2. See this volume, p. 158, n. 11.

3. Michel Foucault, introduction to *The Normal and the Pathological*, by Georges Canguilhem, trans. Carolyn R. Fawcett (New York: Zone Books, 1991), 7–24 (*DE*, no. 219).

4. *GSO*, 1–23.

5. Michel Foucault, "What Is Revolution?," in *The Politics of Truth*, ed. S. Lotringer, trans. Lysa Hochroth (Los Angeles: Semiotext(e), 2007), 83–95.

6. Michel Foucault, "What Is Enlightenment?," trans. Catherine Porter, in *EW* 1:303–19 (*DE*, no. 339).

7. This volume, p. 63.

8. Michel Foucault, *Introduction to Kant's Anthropology*, trans. Roberto Nigro and Kate Briggs (Cambridge, MA: MIT Press, 2008).

9. *STP*, 108.

10. See *STP*, 115–226.

11. See Daniel Defert, "Chronology," in *A Companion to Foucault*, ed. Christopher Falzon, Timothy O'Leary, and Jana Sawicki, trans. Timothy O'Leary (Chichester: Wiley-Blackwell, 2013), 66.

12. Foucault, introduction to *On the Normal and the Pathological*, 12.

13. The theme of "philosophical journalism" associated with Kant's

text on the Enlightenment comes up again in an article published in April 1979. (See Michel Foucault, "For an Ethic of Discomfort," in *EW* 3:443 [*DE*, no. 266]), but disappears completely in later texts, perhaps also because of the controversies that followed Foucault's reports on the Iranian revolution. See also this volume, p. 159, n. 13.

14. Foucault, introduction to *On the Normal and the Pathological*, 10–11.

15. See Defert, "Chronology," 67.

16. See this volume, p. 156, n. 1.

17. This volume, p. 19.

18. This volume, p. 48.

19. This problem was examined by Frédéric Gros and Philippe Sabot in two valuable articles: Frédéric Gros, "Foucault et la leçon kantienne des Lumières," *Lumières* 8 (2006): 159–67, and Philippe Sabot, "Ouverture: Critique, attitude critique, résistance," in *Michel Foucault. À l'épreuve du pouvoir*, ed. Édouard Jolly and Philippe Sabot (Villeneuve-d'Ascq: Presses Universitaires du Septentrion, 2013), 13–26.

20. This volume, p. 48.

21. See Michel Foucault, "What Is an Author?," in *EW* 2:205–22 (*DE*, no. 69 and 258).

22. This volume, p. 48. In the Western tradition, we are well aware that the epistemological-transcendental question merits philosophical treatment. But on the other hand, the critical attitude emerges more as a sociological object, not deserving of "the lofty and profound gaze of the philosopher." See Michel Foucault, "Nietzsche, Genealogy, History," in *EW* 2:370 (*DE*, no. 84).

23. This volume, p. 26.

24. Today we run the risk of forgetting that this text by Kant was completely unknown at the time Foucault was speaking and as a consequence missing the subversiveness of his choice, a choice aimed at destroying the traditional distinction between important works and insignificant works. On this philosophical attitude, which he shared with Bachelard, see Michel Foucault, "Piéger sa propre culture," in *DE* I, no. 111, p. 1250.

25. This volume, pp. 21–22.

26. See *STP*, 163–85.

27. This volume, p. 24. This formulation could open up the possibility of tracing a link between what Foucault describes here as the "critical attitude" and what he later described as "critical governmental reason" in the first lecture of his course at the Collège de France *The Birth of Biopolitics*. Indeed, in describing the emergence of liberalism, Foucault emphasizes the "self-limitation of governmental reason" which characterizes it and which revolves around "how not to govern too much." See Michel Foucault, *The Birth of Biopolitics: Lectures at the Collège de France, 1978–1979*, ed. Michel Senellart, trans. Graham Burchell, English series ed. Arnold I. Davidson (London: Palgrave Macmillan, 2008), 12–13, 20. However, this analogy is only superficial and generally misleading, as liberalism itself is a specific way of governing, and so it is always possible to oppose it with the refusal to be governed *in this way*. Self-limitation is not a *counter*-conduct.

28. *STP*, 193–95.

29. This volume, p. 56.

30. In fact, Foucault is not intending to refer to "something like a fundamental anarchism, or an originary freedom that was absolutely and fundamentally resistant to any governmentalization." See this volume, p. 56.

31. This volume, p. 24, n. *, and pp. 26–27, n. *.

32. This volume, p. 24–25. See also *STP*, 213.

33. This volume, p. 50.

34. This volume, p. 26, n. *.

35. This volume, p. 26.

36. See *GSO*, 30–33 and Foucault, "What Is Enlightenment?," 307–8.

37. This volume, p. 29.

38. This volume, p. 31.

39. This volume, p. 36 and p. 160, n. 20.

40. At the end of his article on Kant and the Aufklärung published in the United States in 1984, Foucault raises a number of methodological points but much more broadly. See Foucault, "What Is Enlightenment?," 312–18.

41. See Michel Foucault, "Questions of Method," in *EW* 3:223–38 (*DE*, no. 278).

42. This volume, pp. 36, 38.

43. See for example *GSO*, 2–5. Michel Foucault, "Preface to *The History of Sexuality*, Volume Two," in *EW* 1:202–5 (*DE*, no. 345); "'Foucault' by Maurice Florence," in *EW* 2:459–64 (*DE*, no. 345).

44. See *CT*, 174. In 1984, Foucault mounted a similar argument that the historico-critical investigations that needed to be undertaken within the framework of what he calls the "critical ontology of ourselves" have been general and recurrent. This does not mean that we should retrace their supposed "metahistorical continuity through time [. . .]. What must be grasped is the extent to which what we know of it, the forms of power that are exercised in it, and the experience that we have in it of ourselves constitute nothing but determined historical figures, through a certain form of problematization that defines objects, rules of action, modes of relation to oneself." See Foucault, "What Is Enlightenment?," 318–19.

45. In the debate that followed the lecture to the Société française de Philosophie, Foucault suggested that the question of the Aufklärung could be used to gather up "all possible history right back to the primordial origins of philosophy. So you could, I think, validly examine Socrates's trial without anachronism, but on the basis of a problem which is, and which was in any case perceived by Kant, as being a problem related to the Aufklärung." See this volume, p. 55.

46. [The problem of translating the words *connaissance* and *savoir* into English is a difficult one in relation to Foucault's work. Both words translate as "knowledge." For comments by Foucault in 1978 on the difference, see this volume, p. 162, n. 26. See also Foucault's *The Archaeology of Knowledge*, where the English translator, Alan Sheridan, explains the difference in a footnote: "*Connaissance* refers [. . .] to a particular corpus of knowledge, a particular discipline—biology or economics, for example. *Savoir*, which is usually defined as knowledge in general, the totality of *connaissance*, is used by Foucault in an underlying, rather than an overall, way. He has himself offered the following comment on his usage of the terms: 'By *connaissance* I mean the relation of the subject to the object and the formal rules that govern it. *Savoir* refers to the conditions that are necessary in a particular period for this or that type of object to be given to *connaissance* and for this or that type of enunciation to be formulated'" (*AK*, 16–17, n. 3).—Trans.]

47. This volume, pp. 38–42.

48. This volume, pp. 42–46. In 1983 during the discussion with the Department of History at the University of California, Berkeley, which took place shortly after the lecture "The Culture of Self," Foucault asserted that he had "never stopped doing archaeology" and "never stopped doing genealogy." Nonetheless, we are obliged to note that his definitions of archaeology and genealogy changed over the years, adapting to the specific contexts of his analyses. See this volume, p. 100. See also this volume, pp. 163–65, nn. 30 and 32.

49. This volume, p. 47.

50. See *GSO*, 15–20.

51. See this volume, p. 167, n. 5.

52. This volume, p. 65.

53. This volume, p. 66.

54. *GSO*, 20–21. In the Howison Lectures delivered at Berkeley in October 1980, Foucault traces an opposition which seems to anticipate these formulations. He says, "It is a question of searching for another kind of critical philosophy. Not a critical philosophy that seeks to determine the conditions and the limits of our possible knowledge of the object, but a critical philosophy that seeks the conditions and the indefinite possibilities of transforming the subject, of transforming ourselves." See *ABHS*, 24, n. b.

55. This volume, p. 66.

56. In the first version of the introduction to *The Use of Pleasure*, Foucault similarly defines critique as "an analysis of the historical conditions that bear on the creation of links to truth, to rules and to the self." See Foucault, "Preface to *The History of Sexuality*, Volume Two," 201. [This text was an early version of the introduction to *The Use of Pleasure* and was originally published in Michel Foucault, *The Foucault Reader*, ed. Paul Rabinow (New York: Vintage, 1984). It is substantially different from the introduction that finally appeared in *UP*.—Trans.]

57. This volume, p. 67. During the debate with the Department of Philosophy at the University of California, Berkeley, which took place shortly after the lecture "The Culture of Self," Foucault explained that in fact, he found that "at least in our societies [. . .] the relation to the self is constituted in large part within the field of sexual experience." It would therefore be "quite impossible to dissociate the problem of the constitution of the self and the problem of the history of sexuality."

See this volume, p. 93. For a similar argument introducing the theme of techniques of the self, see *ABHS*, 34–35; Michel Foucault, "Sexuality and Solitude," in *EW* 1:179–80 (*DE*, no. 295); Michel Foucault, "The Political Technology of Individuals," in *EW* 3:403–4 (*DE*, no. 364).

58. See *HIST*, 51–131.

59. See Michel Foucault, "The Subject and Power," in *EW* 3:327 (*DE*, no. 306): "It is not power, but the subject, that is the general theme of my research."

60. This volume, pp. 70–71. As Foucault explains in his discussion with the Department of Philosophy, he uses the word "culture" because the culture of the self "was not just a philosophical idea, but it really was a practice"—it was a notion, a set of techniques, a type of experience and a social activity all at once. This volume, pp. 84, 89–90. See also this volume, pp. 108–11, where Foucault stresses the "autonomy" of this Greco-Latin culture of the self: Caring for oneself in antiquity was a personal choice that was not necessarily linked to religious, political, or educational institutions.

61. Foucault, "The Political Technology of Individuals," 403.

62. *GSO*, 6–7.

63. Even if Foucault defines modernity in this piece as "as an attitude rather than a period of history," analogous to "what the Greeks called an *ēthos*." He characterizes it, among other things, as an "indispensable asceticism" through which one takes oneself as "the object of a complex and difficult elaboration." See Foucault, "What Is Enlightenment?," 309, 311.

64. *GSO*, 350.

65. Michel Foucault, *"Discourse and Truth" and "Parrēsia,"* ed. Henri-Paul Fruchaud and Daniele Lorenzini, English edition established by Nancy Luxon (Chicago: University of Chicago Press, 2019), 63.

66. This volume, p. 139.

67. See *HS*, 491–505.

68. See *CS*, 39–68. [The English translation originally published in 1984 translates this as "The Cultivation of the Self." The subsequent convention in English language studies of Foucault has been to translate this phrase as "The Culture of the Self."—Trans.]

69. This volume, pp. 70–71.

70. *CS*, 43–44. See also *HS*, 179–80, 205.

71. This volume, p. 72.

72. See *HS* 32–46, 50–58, 65–78, and passim. See also Michel Foucault, "Technologies of the Self," in *EW* 1:228–31 (*DE*, no. 363).

73. This volume, p. 74. On the "ontological knowledge of the self as a soul," in Plato, and on the very different meaning that *gnōthi seauton* takes on in late Stoicism (defining a "whole other style of relationship to the self"), see also this volume, pp. 130–34.

74. For a description of the notable features of the culture of the self in the first two centuries AD, see also, e.g., *HS*, 81, and *CS*, 43–68.

75. This volume, p. 75.

76. This volume, p. 77.

77. This volume, p. 79.

78. Furthermore, Foucault argues that the new features of the culture of the self in the first two centuries AD also go on to characterize "Christian care of the self" and, in a way, "our own culture of the self." See this volume, p. 74. In the discussion with the Department of French, however, he points out that there were also very significant transformations of the ancient experience of the self within Christianity. This volume, p. 120. See also this volume, p. 185, n. 100.

79. See this volume, p. 82.

80. This volume, pp. 87, 86, 89. See also pp. 144–45. "The practice of the self [. . .] is the way in which the individual, in the relation he has to himself or herself, constructs him or herself as a subject. [. . .] You create yourself as subject in relation to the self, the subject is not a given."

81. See *ABHS*, 76.

82. This volume, p. 82.

83. Michel Foucault, "So Is It Important to Think?," in *EW* 3:458 (*DE*, no. 296).

84. See *UP*, 27–28.

85. Foucault, "The Subject and Power," 335.

86. See Foucault, "Michel Foucault et Gilles Deleuze veulent rendre à Nietzsche son vrai visage," *DE I*, no. 41, 579: "Nietzsche's appearance constitutes a break in the history of Western thought. With him the mode of philosophical discourse changed. Previously, this discourse was an anonymous *I*. Thus, the *Meditations on First Philosophy* have a subjective character. But the reader can take the place of Descartes. Impossible to say 'I' in Nietzsche's place."

87. Foucault, "The Subject and Power," 335, 336.

88. Foucault, "What Is Enlightenment?," 319.

89. This volume, p. 112. For similar reasoning, see also Discussion with Michel Foucault, Institut Mémoires de l'édition contemporaine (IMEC) / Fonds Michel Foucault, D 250 (5), pp. 5–6.

What Is Critique?

1. After the last lecture of his course at the Collège de France *Security, Territory, Population*, delivered on April 5, 1978, Foucault went to Japan and stayed until the end of that month. See Daniel Defert, "Chronology," in *A Companion to Foucault*, ed. Christopher Falzon, Timothy O'Leary, and Jana Sawicki, trans. Timothy O'Leary (Chichester: Wiley-Blackwell, 2013), 67. During his visit he gave several important lectures and took part in numerous discussions and interviews. See Michel Foucault, "Sexualité et politique" (entretien avec C. Nemoto et M. Watanabe), *DE II*, no. 230, pp. 522–31; "La société disciplinaire en crise," in *DE II*, no. 231, pp. 532–34; "The Analytic Philosophy of Politics," trans. Giovanni Mascaretti, *Foucault Studies* 24 (2018): 188–200 (*DE*, no. 232); "Sexuality and Power," in *Religion and Culture*, ed. Jeremy Carrette, trans. Richard A. Lynch (Manchester: Manchester University Press, 1999), 115–30 (*DE*, no. 233); "The Philosophical Scene: Foucault Interviewed by Moriaki Watanabe," in *Foucault's Theatres*, ed. Tony Fisher and Kélina Gotman, trans. Robert Bononno (Manchester: Manchester University Press, 2020), 221–38 (*DE*, no. 234); "Méthodologie pour la connaissance du monde: comment se débarrasser du marxisme," (Interview with R. Yoshimoto), in *DE II*, no. 235, pp. 595–618; "Michel Foucault and Zen: A Stay in a Zen Temple," in *Religion and Culture*, ed. Jeremy Carrette, trans. Richard Townsend (Manchester: Manchester University Press, 1999), 110–14 (*DE*, no. 236).

2. See Michel Foucault, "What Is an Author?," in *EW* 2, 205–22.

3. Foucault studied pastoral power as a "matrix" of the government of people for the first time in his course at the Collège de France *Security, Territory, Population*, particularly in the lectures delivered between February 8 and March 1, 1978. See *STP*, 123–216. In this context, Foucault focuses on the Hebrew theme of the pastorate before approaching the Christian pastorate. See *STP*, 123–29. For a more detailed account of Foucault's explanations as to why the shepherd-flock relationship was not considered a good political model in Greco-Roman antiquity, see *STP*,

136–48. Foucault returns several times to the analysis of pastoral power between 1978 and 1979. See Foucault, "The Analytic Philosophy of Politics," 197–99; "Sexuality and Power," 122–26; "Omnes et singulatim: Toward a Critique of Political Reason," in *EW* 3:298–325 (*DE*, no. 291). See also Foucault, "The Subject and Power," in *EW* 3:333–35 (*DE*, no. 306).

4. In the lecture on February 22, 1978, delivered as part of his Collège de France course *Security, Territory, Population*, Foucault organized his analysis of the Christian pastorate and its specificity with regards to the Hebrew theme of the shepherd around three axes: the relation to salvation, the relation to the law (the instance of "pure obedience"), and the relation to the truth. See *STP*, 166–84. These three elements are found more broadly and sometimes with differences of emphasis, (as is the case here, in the presentation to the Société française de Philosophie) on all the other occasions Foucault addresses the Christian pastorate.

5. See *GL*, 51, and *GL*, 68, n. 9.

6. On the "explosion" of the art of governing people beyond the religious realm, see *STP*, 229–39 and Foucault, "The Analytic Philosophy of Politics," 198–99.

7. [The phrase Foucault uses in French is "*l'art de ne pas être tellement gouverné.*" This phrase is ambiguous in English and can be translated in different ways as "the art of not being governed so much" but also "the art of not being governed in this/that way." The phrase has been rendered in previous translations and commentaries in English as "the art of not being governed quite so much," so this form will be retained here to facilitate scholarly work tracking this concept in English.—Trans.]

8. In the lecture of March 1, 1978, delivered as part of his course at the Collège de France *Security, Territory, Population*, Foucault analyzes five principal forms of "pastoral counter-conducts" in the Middle Ages, including the "problem of Scripture," namely "the return to the texts, to Scripture" with an antipastoral aim. See *STP*, 204, 213. In the discussion after his presentation to the Société française de Philosophie, Foucault also mentioned mysticism as "one of the first great forms of revolt in the West" (this volume, pp. 56–57). For a more detailed analysis of mysticism as a "form of counter-conduct," see *STP*, 212–13. On three forms of counterconduct "in the modern system of governmentality" (revolutionary eschatology, the absolute right to revolt, the nation as a principle that opposes the state), see *STP*, 355–57.

9. For an analogous definition of critique "understood as analysis of the historical conditions that bear on the creation of links to truth, to rules and to the self," see Michel Foucault, "Preface to *The History of Sexuality*, Volume Two," in *EW* 1:201 (*DE*, no. 345).

10. For previous uses of this expression the "politics of truth," see in 1976, *HIST*, 60, and in 1978, Michel Foucault, "Truth and Power," in *EW* 3:131 (*DE*, no. 192).

11. See Immanuel Kant, "An Answer to the Question: What Is Enlightenment?," in *Practical Philosophy*, ed. Mary J. Gregor, 11–22, The Cambridge Edition of the Works of Immanuel Kant (Cambridge: Cambridge University Press, 1996), 11–22. In addition to his presentation to the Société française de Philosophie, Foucault deals at length with this text by Kant in the first lecture of his course at the Collège de France *The Government of Self and of Others* (See *GSO*, 6–39). A part of this was taken up and published in the form of an article in *Magazine Littéraire* in 1984. See Michel Foucault, "What Is Revolution?," in *The Politics of Truth*, ed. S. Lotringer, trans. Lysa Hochroth (Los Angeles: Semiotext(e), 2007), 83–95 (*DE*, no. 351), and "What Is Enlightenment?," trans. Catherine Porter, in *EW* 1:303–19 (*DE*, no. 339). He also refers to it on several other occasions: See Foucault, introduction to *The Normal and the Pathological*, by Georges Canguilhem, trans. Carolyn R. Fawcett (New York: Zone Books, 1991), 9–12 (*DE*, no. 219). "For an Ethic of Discomfort," in *EW* 3:443 (*DE*, no. 266); "Postface," in *DE II*, no. 279, 855–56; "The Subject and Power," 328, 335–36; "Structuralism and Post-Structuralism," in *EW* 2:439–40, 442, 449 (*DE*, no. 330); "Life: Experience and Science," in *EW* 2:467–68 (*DE*, no. 361); "The Political Technology of Individuals," in *EW* 3:403 (*DE*, no. 364). See also Foucault, "The Culture of the Self," this volume, pp. 64–66, and the extract from a debate after the Tanner Lecture Foucault gave at the University of Stanford in October 1979, this volume, pp. 167–69, n. 5.

12. See Kant, "An Answer to the Question: What Is Enlightenment?," 8:35 (p. 17). "*Enlightenment is the human being's emergence from his self-incurred minority*. Minority is inability to make use of one's own understanding without direction from another. This minority *is self-incurred* when its cause lies not in lack of understanding but in lack of resolution and courage to use it without direction from another. *Sapere aude!* Have courage to make use of your *own* understanding! is thus the

motto of enlightenment." For a more detailed commentary on this first paragraph of Kant's article, see *GSO*, 26–39.

13. In the January 1978 introduction to the American translation of Georges Canguilhem's book *The Normal and the Pathological*, Foucault states that the texts published by Moses Mendelssohn and Kant in the *Berlinische Monatsschrift* in 1784 "inaugurated a 'philosophical journalism' which, along with university teaching, was one of the major forms of the institutional implantation of philosophy in the nineteenth century." In this introduction, however, Foucault explicitly links the theme of "philosophical journalism" to the problem of the analysis of the "'present' moment," a problem he leaves aside in his presentation to the Société française de Philosophie. See Foucault, introduction to *The Normal and the Pathological*, 10. See also "For an Ethic of Discomfort," in *EW* 3:443 (*DE*, no. 266): "Should this singular inquiry be placed in the history of journalism or of philosophy? I only know that, since that time, there have not been many philosophies that don't revolve around the question: 'What are we now? What is this ever so fragile moment from which we cannot detach our identity and which will carry that identity away with it?' But I believe this question is also the basis of the journalist's occupation. The concern to say what is happening [. . .] is not so much prompted by the desire to know always and everywhere what makes this happening possible but, rather, by the desire to make out what is concealed under that precise, floating, mysterious, utterly simple word 'today.'" In revisiting and modifying his introduction to the American translation of *The Normal and the Pathological* for a special issue of the *Revue de métaphysique et de morale* in April 1984 dedicated to Canguilhem, Foucault continued to stress the question of the present moment and contemporary reality but decided to delete the reference to "philosophical journalism." See Foucault, "Life: Experience and Science," 468.

14. See Kant, "An Answer to the Question: What Is Enlightenment?," 8:35 (p. 17) 8:41 (pp. 21–22).

15. See Kant, "An Answer to the Question: What Is Enlightenment?," 8:35 (p. 17) 8:41 (p. 22).See also *GSO*, 38 and Foucault, "What Is Enlightenment?," 305–6.

16. The same confrontation of the "destiny" of the question of Aufklärung in Germany and in France is also found in Foucault, in-

troduction to *The Normal and the Pathological*, 10–13, where Foucault argues that "German philosophy gave it a substance above all in a historical and political reflection on society," while "in France it is the history of science which has above all served to support the philosophical question of the Enlightenment." See also Michel Foucault, "Structuralism and Poststructuralism," in *EW* 2:439–40, and "Life: Experience and Science," 468–70.

17. See Edmund Husserl, *The Crisis of European Sciences and Transcendental Phenomenology: An Introduction to Phenomenological Philosophy*, trans. David Carr (Evanston: Northwestern University Press, 1970).

18. See Jean-Paul Sartre, *Nausea*, trans. Robert Baldick (London: Penguin, 2000 [1938]).

19. Foucault very clearly distances himself from "polemics" and the "polemicist" in his discussion in "Polemics, Politics and Problematizations: An Interview with Michel Foucault," in *EW* 1:111–14 (*DE*, no. 342).

20. In his texts on Kant and the question of the Aufklärung, Foucault repeatedly claims that his own work is close to that of the Frankfurt School. See *GSO*, 21; Foucault, "What Is Revolution?," 195; "The Political Technology of Individuals," 403. See also the extract from the debate organized after the Tanner Lectures at Stanford (this volume, pp. 167–69, n. 5), where Foucault claims to be part of the same "philosophical family" as the Frankfurt School, and the interview "Structuralism and Poststructuralism," 440, where he goes so far as to say "if I had been familiar with the Frankfurt School, if I had been aware of it at the time, I would not have said a number of stupid things that I did say, and I would have avoided many of the detours I made while trying to pursue my own humble path."

21. In his response to Maurice Agulhon, published as a postface to *L'impossible prison. Recherches sur le système pénitentiaire en XIXe siècle*, ed. Michelle Perrot (Paris: Seuil, 1980), 223–38, (republished as "Postface," in *DE II*, no. 279, 856), Foucault suggests starting "a great historical investigation" into the way in which the Aufklärung—"our most 'current past'"—was "perceived, thought about, lived, imagined, staved off, anathematized and reactivated in nineteenth and twentieth century Europe." In this connection he speaks of an "interesting 'historico-philosophical' work where the relations between historians and philosophers could be tested."

22. In an interview in 1979, Foucault claimed he was practicing "a kind of historical fiction," which a historian could therefore legitimately criticize, because "what I say is not true," but Foucault explains that he is trying to "provoke an interference between our reality and the knowledge of our past history" in order to produce "real effects on our present history." He hopes that "the truth" of his books will be "in the future." See Michel Foucault, "Truth Is in the Future," in *FL*, 301 (*DE*, no. 272, and *DE*, no. 280). On this notion of historical fiction, see also Michel Foucault, "The History of Sexuality: Interview with Lucette Finas," in *Power/Knowledge: Selected Interviews and Other Writings, 1972–1977*, ed. C. Gordon, trans. Leo Marshall (New York: Pantheon, 1980), 193 (*DE*, no. 197) and "Interview with Michel Foucault," in *EW* 3:243 (*DE*, no. 281).

23. In his 1984 article on Kant and the Aufklärung published in the United States, Foucault proposed to "envisage modernity as an attitude rather than as a period of history"—that is, as "a mode of relating to contemporary reality; a voluntary choice made by certain people; in the end, a way of thinking and feeling; a way too of acting and behaving that at one and the same time marks a relation of belonging and presents itself as a task." See Foucault, "What Is Enlightenment?," 309.

24. The analysis of the relationships between power, truth, and the subject is at the heart of Foucault's work in the 1970s and 1980s, to the extent that in 1983 and 1984 Foucault retrospectively reconstructed his own intellectual journey by organizing it around these three poles or "axes." See for example *GSO*, 3–6 and Michel Foucault, "Preface to *The History of Sexuality*, Volume Two," in *EW* 1:201. It is also very significant that Foucault, in the inaugural lecture of his course at the Collège de France *The Courage of Truth*, presents his study of *parrēsia* precisely as a way of analyzing how "the modes of veridiction, the study of techniques of governmentality, and the identification of forms of practice of self interweave"—that is, a way of studying "the relations between truth, power, and subject without ever reducing each of them to the others." See *CT*, 8–9.

25. Eventalization as a "breach of self-evidence, of those self-evidences on which our knowledges, acquiescences and practices rest" and as an instrument of "the multiplication or pluralization of causes" throws into question any ideas of unique necessity and constitutes for Foucault "the point at issue, both in historical analysis and in political

critique." See Michel Foucault, "Questions of Method," *EW* 3:226–29 (*DE*, no. 278).

26. In an interview conducted at the end of 1978, Foucault proposed a somewhat different distinction between *savoir* and *connaissance*. "I use the word '*savoir*' ['knowledge'] while drawing a distinction between it and the word '*connaissance*' ['knowledge']. I see '*savoir*' as a process by which the subject undergoes a modification through the very things that one knows [*connaît*] or, rather, in the course of the work that one does in order to know. It is what enables one both to modify the subject and to construct the object. *Connaissance* is the work that makes it possible to multiply the knowable objects, to manifest their intelligibility, to understand their rationality, while maintaining the fixity of the inquiring subject." And Foucault adds: "With the idea of archaeology it's precisely a matter of recapturing the construction of a *connaissance* that is of a relation between a fixed subject and a domain of objects, in its historical roots, in this movement of *savoir* which makes the construction possible." See Foucault, "Interview with Michel Foucault," 256.

27. In a 1984 interview, Foucault clearly explains his distinction between power and domination. "Power relations" are "strategic games between liberties," which means that "some try to control the conduct of others, who in turn try to avoid allowing their conduct to be controlled or try to control the conduct of the other." These relationships are therefore "mobile, reversible and unstable," and presuppose a certain form, a certain measure of freedom for individuals. In contrast in "states of domination" ("that people ordinarily call "power,"") power relations "are fixed in such a way that they are perpetually asymmetrical and allow an extremely limited margin of freedom." See Michel Foucault, "The Ethics of the Concern of the Self as a Practice of Freedom," in *EW* 1:283, 299, 292 (*DE*, no. 356). See also Foucault, "The Subject and Power," 340–42. In a discussion with Hubert Dreyfus and Paul Rabinow at Berkeley in April 1983, Foucault upheld the same idea, but rather than discussing "states of domination," he spoke of "relationships of violence." "In relationships of violence, you cannot do anything, you are forced because you are tied up ... Well, in a power relation, for one of the two parties there is always the possibility to say no, escaping, resisting, and so on. [. . .] I would say that the simplest definition of power relations is this one: when someone tries to govern the actions

of others. Of course, you can govern the action of another by taking his hand and forcing him to move in a particular way—that's violence, not power. Power starts when you try to govern the action of others, the behavior of others, without using violence, which doesn't mean that you don't use the threat of violence and in some cases, violence will really be used, in order to make an example at least and so on. So, it's true that violence is directly linked to power, but I think that power starts when you don't use violence, at least to begin with. And in this case, resistance begins with power, or the possibility of resistance begins with power." See Discussion with Michel Foucault, IMEC / Fonds Michel Foucault, D 250 (7), pp. 15, 22–23.

28. See Michel Foucault, "Penal Theories and Institutions," in *EW* 1:17 (*DE*, no. 115). "No knowledge is formed without a system of communication, registration, accumulation, and displacement that is in itself a form of power linked, in its existence and its functioning, to other forms of power. No power, on the other hand, is exercised without the extraction, appropriation, distribution or restraint of a knowledge. At this level, there is not knowledge [*connaissance*] on one side, and society on the other, or science and the state, but the basic forms of 'power-knowledge' ['*pouvoir-savoir*']."

29. On the concept of positivity, see *AK*, 141.

30. In 1969, in *The Archaeology of Knowledge*, Foucault uses the term "archaeology," to designate "the general theme of a description that questions the already-said at the level of its existence: of the enunciative function that operates within it, of the discursive formation, and the general archive system to which it belongs." An analysis of this type, Foucault specifies, "does not imply the search for a beginning." See *AK*, 148, and, more generally, the whole of part 4, "Archaeological Description," 150–215. See also Michel Foucault, "The Archaeology of Knowledge," in *FL*, 57 (*DE*, no. 66); "The Birth of a World," in *FL*, 65, (*DE*, no. 68); "Dialogue on Power," in Simeon Wade, "Chez Foucault" (self-pub., 1978), 10–11, (*DE*, no. 221). It is also significant that in 1971, in responding to George Steiner's criticisms of *The Order of Things*, Foucault specifies that the term "archaeology" is found in Kant, who "used this word in order to designate the history of that which renders necessary a certain form of thought." See Michel Foucault, "Monstrosities in Criticism," *Diacritics* 1, no. 1 (1971): 60 (*DE*, no. 97.) Foucault is referring to Kant's

text, "What Real Progress Has Metaphysics Made in Germany since the Time of Leibniz and Wolff? (1793/1804)," in *Theoretical Philosophy after 1781*, ed. Henry Allison and Peter Heath, trans. Gary Hatfield and Michael Friedman, 337–424, The Cambridge Edition of the Works of Immanuel Kant (Cambridge: Cambridge University Press, 2002). Foucault also uses the term "archaeology" to designate our a priori, which, in contrast to Kant, are always historical a priori—namely, "events." In the 1984 article on Kant and the Aufklärung published in the United States, Foucault states that critique, understood as "a historical investigation into the events that have led us to constitute ourselves and to recognize ourselves as subjects of what we are doing, thinking, saying" is "genealogical in its design and archaeological in its method." It is archaeological because "it will not seek to identify the universal structures of all knowledge [*connaissance*], or of all possible moral action, but will seek to treat the instances of discourse that articulate what we think, say, and do as so many historical events." See Foucault, "What Is Enlightenment?," 315. See also "Discussion with the Department of History," this volume, pp. 95–97, 100.

31. On the notion of singularity, as always linked to the notion of the event, see Foucault, "Questions of Method," 226, and "Preface to *The History of Sexuality*, Volume Two," 199–200. See also Michel Foucault, "Theatrum Philosophicum," in *EW* 2:350 (*DE*, no. 80).

32. In 1971, drawing inspiration from Nietzsche, Foucault was already explaining that the goal of genealogy was not to "describe a linear development," but "it must record the singularity of events, outside of any monotonous finality; it must seek them in the most unpromising places, in what we tend to feel is without history [. . .]; it must be sensitive to their recurrence, not in order to trace the gradual curve of their evolution, but to isolate the different scenes where they engaged in different roles. Finally, genealogy must define even those instances when they were absent, the moment when they remained unrealized." Genealogy is therefore radically opposed to the search for "origin." See Foucault, "Nietzsche, Genealogy, History," *EW* 2:369 (*DE*, no. 84). In the 1984 article on Kant and the Aufklärung published in the United States, while arguing that critique is "genealogical in its design and archaeological in its method" (see this volume, p. 164, n. 30), Foucault specifies that it is genealogical because it "will not deduce from the form of what we are

what it is impossible for us to do and to know; but it will separate out, from the contingency that has made us what we are, the possibility of no longer being, doing or thinking what we are, do, or think." See Foucault, "What Is Enlightenment?," 315–16. See also this volume, pp. 95–97, 100.

33. See *AK*, part 2, chap. 6, "The Formation of Strategies," 71–78.

34. See this volume, pp. 162–63, n. 27.

35. On the theme of antipastoral struggles, see *STP*, 193–216, and "Omnes et singulatim," 312–13.

36. In 1984, responding to a question relating to the task of philosophy, Foucault stated: "In its critical aspect—I mean critical in a broad sense—philosophy is that which calls into question domination at every level and in every form in which it exists, whether political, economic, sexual, institutional or what have you. To a certain extent, this critical function of philosophy derives from the Socratic imperative: 'Take care of yourself,' in other words, 'Make freedom your foundation, through the mastery of yourself.'" See Foucault, "The Ethics of the Concern of the Self as a Practice of Freedom," 300–301.

37. See this volume, p. 157, n. 8.

38. Foucault had mentioned this "problem of the will" a month earlier in an interview conducted in Japan. Here he argued that Western philosophy had dealt with the will in two ways only: first using the model of natural philosophy (nature-force) and second using the model of the philosophy of law (good and evil). And even if this scheme of thought underwent a rupture with Schopenhauer and Nietzsche, Foucault was convinced that "Western philosophy has always been incapable of thinking about the question of the will in a relevant fashion." He then suggested borrowing a method from military strategy to pose the question of will "as struggle, using a strategic point of view to analyze conflict when various antagonisms develop." See Foucault, "Méthodologie pour la connaissance du monde," 603–5.

39. See Plato, *Protagoras*, trans. Stanley Lombardo and Karen Bell, in *Complete Works*, ed. John M. Cooper and D. S. Hutchinson (Indianapolis: Hackett, 1997), 320c–324d (pp. 756–59).

40. See Kant, "An Answer to the Question: What Is Enlightenment?," 8:37–38 (pp. 18–19). For a more detailed commentary on the Kantian distinction between the public and private use of reason, see *GSO*, 34–39, and Foucault, "What Is Enlightenment?," 307–8.

41. See Immanuel Kant, *Religion within the Bounds of Bare Reason*, trans. Werner S. Pluhar (Cambridge, MA: Hackett, 2009), 57, 137n327, 198–99. [The English translator uses the word "enlightenment." See his translator's note, p. 57, n. 3.—Trans.]

42. It was only in the discussion that followed his presentation to the Société française de Philosophie in 1978 that Foucault raised the question of the Aufklärung as a contemporary reality to which Kant felt bound and questioned himself about in his text. This question, however, went on to play a major role in Foucault's other discussions on Kant and the Aufklärung. Between 1983 and 1984, he argued that Kant's text had inaugurated a whole critical tradition that he labelled an "ontology of ourselves," which was at the same time an "ontology of the present" or an "ontology of present reality." See *GSO*, 21, and Foucault, "What Is Revolution?," 95 (trans. mod.). It is also significant that, in an interview conducted in Japan in April 1978, Foucault argued that Nietzsche was the first "to define philosophy as an activity that helps us determine what is going on and what is going on now" ("philosophy of the present, philosophy of the event, philosophy of what is happening"). He attributed the role of "diagnostician" of present reality [*actualité*] to Nietzsche. See Foucault, "The Philosophical Scene," 223.

The Culture of the Self

1. Lucian, "Hermotimus, or Concerning the Sects," in *Lucian*, vol. 6, trans. K. Kilburn, Loeb Classical Library (Cambridge, MA: Harvard University Press, 1959), 259–415. Foucault had already mentioned this text by Lucian in the January 20, 1982, lecture of his course at the Collège de France *The Hermeneutics of the Subject*, and he also returns to it more briefly in "The Concern for the Self." See *HS*, 92–93, and *CS*, 49–50.

2. Immanuel Kant, "An Answer to the Question: What Is Enlightenment? (1784)," in *Practical Philosophy*, ed. Mary J. Gregor, 11–22, The Cambridge Edition of the Works of Immanuel Kant (Cambridge: Cambridge University Press, 1996).

3. See Moses Mendelssohn, "On the Question: What Does 'To Enlighten' Mean?," in *Philosophical Writings*, ed. and trans. Daniel O. Dahlstrom (Cambridge: Cambridge University Press, 1997), 311–17.

4. On the encounter between the philosophical Aufklärung and the Haskalah, or "Jewish Aufklärung," see *GSO*, 9, and Michel Foucault, "What Is Enlightenment?," trans. Catherine Porter, in *EW* 1:304 (*DE*, no. 339). On the Haskalah, see also *GSO*, 22, n. 12.

5. The discussion of Kant's article in light of the emergence of this philosophical interrogation of the present, contemporary reality, and "today"—and on what *we* are at this precise moment in history—is probably the most constant element in the series of texts that Foucault dedicated to "Was ist Aufklärung?" See Michel Foucault, introduction to *The Normal and the Pathological*, by Georges Canguilhem, trans. Carolyn R. Fawcett (New York: Zone Books, 1991), 9–10 (*DE*, no. 219); "For an Ethic of Discomfort," in *EW* 3:443; "The Subject and Power," in *EW* 3:335 (*DE*, no. 306); "Structuralism and Poststructuralism," in *EW* 2:449; "What Is Enlightenment?," 304–5, 310–13; "What Is Revolution?," in *The Politics of Truth*, ed. S. Lotringer, trans. Lysa Hochroth (Los Angeles: Semiotext(e), 2007), 83–90 (*DE*, no. 351); "Life: Experience and Science," in *EW* 2:467–70 (*DE*, no. 361); "The Political Technology of Individuals," in *EW* 3:403 (*DE*, no. 364); *GSO*, 9–15. This interrogation is also at the core of a response by Foucault in a discussion in English following his Tanner Lectures at Stanford in October 1979: "What I would say is that I feel a deep affinity with several German thinkers mainly those in the Frankfurt School. In Germany and France, I think, one of the most important and most constant philosophical problems is the problem of Enlightenment, of Aufklärung, the problem of what happened in the second half of the eighteenth century when something occurred in society and culture, science and literature, as well as in the system of rationality and the system of authority. 'What is Aufklärung?' 'What is Enlightenment?' What does this mean and what are the consequences of this? I think this is still one of the most important philosophical problems. Kant wrote a very interesting text in 1784 titled 'What is Aufklärung?' This is the first time, I think, a philosopher in the history of Western thought, the first time a philosopher has wondered: what's happening today? The introduction of this kind of question into the field of philosophy, the introduction of 'today' as a philosophical category is something that's quite important, quite strange and quite decisive for the history of our philosophy. Before that Descartes,

Spinoza, Leibniz, and even people like Hobbes and Hume—who were deeply interested in their own history, in their own society and much more involved in political problems than Spinoza or Descartes—didn't introduce or formulate the problem in philosophical terms. What is going on today? What is today? What are our present realities? And what are we? And how can we be our own contemporaries? This is Kant's question, and in a certain sense I think it could be possible to reinterpret Kant, even the three *Critiques*, on the basis of this question 'what is Aufklärung?' In a way, even the *Critique of Pure Reason* is a kind of answer to this question 'what is Aufklärung?' and I think that it is possible to demonstrate that the *Critique of Pure Reason* is the answer to this question. Hegel's *The Phenomenology of Spirit*, is nothing other than the answer to the question 'what is Aufklärung?,' with the difference that for him the Aufklärung is a total history of the world. The problem is what is happening now, and what do our contemporary world and its facts mean? This is also Nietzsche's question of course. All of Nietzsche's philosophy and work is aimed at diagnosing what's going on in the present world and what today is. And I think that this kind of philosophical question, which is both historical and political, both historical and topical is quite typical of German thought in the nineteenth and twentieth centuries. I think some French thinkers—[I am not] going to name them—put this philosophical problem in the same terms. [Foucault is probably thinking of Koyré, Bachelard, Cavaillès, and Canguilhem; see Foucault, introduction to *The Normal and the Pathological*, by Georges Canguilhem, 11, and "Life: Experience and Science," 466]. I'd say, at least as far as I'm concerned, if I had to indicate what my philosophical family was, I would say this: my philosophical family is made up of all the philosophers who have nominated the question of the meaning of 'today' or the diagnosis of contemporary reality as the main philosophical question. And in this sense, I feel that I am very close to the people of the Frankfurt School, even if I don't agree with everything they say. The points I have tried to make diverge from the Frankfurt School of course. For instance, with regards to the prison, if I have written a book about the prison, it's because Kirchheimer and Rusche's book, which is a wonderful and very interesting book, doesn't satisfy me on several points. [See Georg Rusche and Otto Kirchheimer, *Punishment*

and Social Structure (London and New York: Routledge, 2003 [1939])].
But that's my family, that's my philosophical family. I would say that
Heidegger is also a philosopher whose main problem is the problem of
what is Aufklärung? In other words, what is the philosophical meaning,
the historical meaning, or the metahistorical meaning of this moment
which is my own present and which is the moment in which I am writing this question? The topicality [*actualité*] of thinking and the relation
between the topicality [*actualité*] of thinking and a very remote event
in the history of thinking, that, I think, is something quite characteristic." See also Discussion with Michel Foucault, IMEC / Fonds Michel Foucault, D 250 (8), pp. 40–41: "In particular, I think that we owe
this critical attitude in general to the Aufklärung, an attitude a certain
number of people share, and I classify myself amongst them. There is a
philosophical task which is the critical analysis of the present. Philosophy usually has the function of being perpetually changing, a function
of the critical analysis of what we are. To this extent, I consider myself
to be totally an heir of the Aufklärung, and not by personal choice,
but because I believe this is the current situation, our present is still
like this."

6. Here and in the lines that follow, Foucault uses the French word. [I
have rendered this word as "contemporary reality" or "present reality"
and included the word *actualité* in brackets. Foucault also uses other
French words in this lecture, which was originally delivered in English
and lightly corrected for English style in this edition. In these instances,
I have included the English word in the main text and added the French
word in brackets and italics.—Trans.]

7. See J. G. Fichte, *Contribution to the Correction of the Public's Judg-
ments on the French Revolution*, ed. and trans. Jeffrey Church and Anna
Marisa Schön (Albany: State University of New York Press, 2021). In
the inaugural lecture of his course at the Collège de France *The Government of Self and Others*, Foucault states that Kant raised the question
of contemporary reality once again, fourteen years after his text on the
Aufklärung, this time in relation to the French Revolution: "What Is
Revolution?" See *GSO*, 15–20, and Foucault, "What Is Revolution?,"
83–90.

8. G. W. F. Hegel, "Hegel to Niethammer, October 13, 1806," in *The*

Letters, trans. Clark Butler and Christiane Seiler, commentary Clark Butler (Bloomington: Indiana University Press, 1984), 114. "I saw the Emperor—this world-soul—riding out of the city on reconnaissance. It is indeed a wonderful sensation to see such an individual, who, concentrated here at a single point, astride a horse, reaches out over the world and masters it."

9. In the inaugural lecture of his course at the Collège de France *The Government of Self and Others*, Foucault likewise maintains that Kant founded "the two great traditions which have divided modern philosophy." On the one hand, we have the "tradition of critical philosophy which raises the question of the conditions of possibility of a true knowledge" (what Foucault calls the "analytic of truth"). On the other, we have the critical tradition which raises the question of present reality and of the "present field of possible experiences" (what Foucault describes as an "ontology of the present, of present reality, an ontology of modernity, an ontology of ourselves.") See *GSO*, 20–21. See also Foucault, "What Is Revolution?," 94–95. In his 1984 article on Kant and the Aufklärung published in the United States, Foucault speaks of a "historical ontology of ourselves" and of a "critical ontology of ourselves," that is an "attitude," a "philosophical ethos that could be described as a permanent critique of our historical era." See Foucault, "What Is Enlightenment?," 316, 319, 312. In the series of lectures that Foucault gave at the University of California, Berkeley, in the fall of 1983, he took the question of how to make sure a statement is true back to the tradition of the analytics of truth. The question, What is the importance of telling the truth, who is able to tell the truth, and why should we tell the truth, know the truth, and recognize who is able to tell the truth? is, Foucault argues, "at the root, at the foundation of what we could call the critical tradition of philosophy in our society." This is why "in analyzing [the] notion of *parrēsia*," Foucault says he "would like also to outline the genealogy of what we could call the critical attitude in our society." See Michel Foucault, *"Discourse and Truth" and "Parrēsia"*, ed. Henri-Paul Fruchaud and Daniele Lorenzini, English edition established by Nancy Luxon (Chicago: The University of Chicago Press, 2019), 224, 63.

10. In his 1984 article on Kant and the Aufklärung published in the United States, Foucault invokes "three axes whose specificity and whose interconnections have to be analyzed" from the perspective of

a "historical ontology of ourselves." "The axis of knowledge, the axis of power, the axis of ethics." See Foucault, "What Is Enlightenment?," 318. Likewise, during a discussion with Hubert Dreyfus and Paul Rabinow at Berkeley in April 1983, Foucault states: "Three domains of genealogy are possible. First, a historical ontology of ourselves in relation to truth through which we constitute ourselves as subjects of knowledge; second, a historical ontology of ourselves in relation to a field of power through which we constitute ourselves as subjects acting on others; third, a historical ontology in relation to ethics through which we constitute ourselves as moral agents." See Michel Foucault, "On the Genealogy of Ethics: An Overview of Work in Progress," in *EW* 1:262 (*DE*, no. 326).

11. See Michel Foucault, "Preface to *The History of Sexuality*, Volume Two," in *EW* 1:200–202 (*DE*, no. 345). For Foucault's project of a "(critical) history of thought," as opposed to the "history of ideas," see among others, Michel Foucault, "Polemics, Politics and Problematizations: An Interview with Michel Foucault," in *EW* 1:117–19 (*DE*, no. 342); "'Foucault' by Maurice Florence," in *EW* 2:463 (*DE*, no. 345); "The Concern for Truth," in *FL*, 456 (*DE*, no. 350).

12. See *ABHS*, 24–26. See also Michel Foucault, "Sexuality and Solitude," in *EW* 1:179–80 (*DE*, no. 295); "Technologies of the Self," in *EW* 1:223–24 (*DE*, no. 363); "The Political Technology of Individuals," 403–4.

13. Foucault is alluding to the three discussions organized in the days following his lecture by the departments of philosophy, history, and French at the University of California, Berkeley, and which are reproduced in this volume.

14. Foucault explicitly places the notion of care of the self (*epimeleia heautou*) at the center of his historico-philosophical investigations, beginning with the inaugural lecture of his course at the Collège de France *The Hermeneutics of the Subject* (see, e.g., *HS*, 2). This notion runs through most of his later works, until the publication in June 1984 of *The Concern for Self*, the third volume of *The History of Sexuality*.

15. Plato, *Apology*, trans. G. M. A. Grube, in *Complete Works*, ed. John M. Cooper and D. S. Hutchinson (Indianapolis: Hackett, 1997), 30a–c (p. 38). For an analysis of three passages of Socrates's *Apology* from the perspective of self-care, see *HS*, 5–9. Foucault also returned to the *Apology* in his lectures at the Collège de France in 1983 and 1984,

but in these the core of his analysis of Plato's text concentrated on Socrates's *parrēsia*. See *GSO*, 311–27, and *CT*, 74–91.

16. See Saint Gregory of Nyssa, "On Virginity," in *St. Gregory: Ascetical Works*, trans. V. W. Callahan, The Fathers of the Church 58 (Washington, DC: Catholic University of America Press, 1967), chap. 13, pp. 46–51. See Foucault, *HS*, 10, 492; "The Ethics of the Concern of the Self as a Practice of Freedom," in *EW* 1:288 (*DE*, no. 356); "Technologies of the Self," 227.

17. See Gregory of Nyssa, "On Virginity," chap. 12, p. 44. See *HS*, 492, and "Technologies of the Self," 227. Foucault also returns to the same chapter 12 of Gregory of Nyssa's "On Virginity" in the last lecture of his course at the Collège de France *The Courage of Truth*, where he focuses on the idea of a "*parrhēsia* of vis-à-vis, of face to face with God." See *CT*, 333.

18. Plutarch, "On the Control of Anger," in *Moralia*, vol. 6, trans. W. C. Helmbold, Loeb Classical Library (Cambridge, MA: Harvard University Press, 1939), 453D (p. 97). "One of those excellent precepts of Musonius which I remember, Sulla, is: 'He that wishes to come through life safe and sound must continue throughout his life to be under treatment.'"

19. See *CS*, 46.

20. See Dio Chrysostom, "Discourse 20. On Retirement," in *Discourses 12–30*, trans. J. W. Cohoon. Loeb Classical Library (Cambridge, MA: Harvard University Press, 1939), 245–69. [Dio of Prusa is also known as Dio Chrysostom.—Trans.]

21. Galen, *On the Passions and Errors of the Soul*, ed. Walther Riese, trans. Paul W. Harkins (Columbus, OH: Ohio State University Press, 1963), 41. "A man does everything, for many years in succession, that he may become a good physician, or public speaker, or grammarian, or geometer. Is it a disgrace for you to toil for a long time that you may one day be a good man?"

22. See Epictetus, *Discourses*, books 1–2, trans. W. A. Oldfather, Loeb Classical Library (Cambridge, MA: Harvard University Press, 1925), book 1, chap. 9, sect. 8–9 (p. 65).

23. See *HS*, 4–5, and Foucault, "Technologies of the Self," 227.

24. The notion of "techniques of the self"—and the historical analysis of these techniques in antiquity—became one of the main axes

of Foucault's research in the 1980s after its introduction in 1980 in his lectures *About the Beginning of the Hermeneutics of the Self* (see *ABHS*, 25). This allowed Foucault "to problematize a subject that is not merely traversed and informed by external governmentalities, but constructs a definite relationship to self by means of regular exercises." See Frédéric Gros, "Course Context," in *ST*, 302. In a lecture given at the University of Vermont in October 1982, Foucault maintains that the "general framework" of the study of technologies of the self is defined by the question formulated by Kant in his text on Aufklärung: "What are we in this time which ours?" See Foucault, "The Political Technology of Individuals," 403.

25. This collective project on the history of technologies of the self in Western societies since ancient Greece found concrete form in the seminar led by Foucault at the University of Vermont in the autumn of 1982. See L. H. Martin, H. Gutman, and P. H. Hutton, eds., *Technologies of the Self: A Seminar with Michel Foucault* (Amherst: University of Massachusetts Press, 1988).

26. See *CS*, 42–43, where Foucault distinguishes three different phenomena within supposed "individualism"—the "individualistic attitude," the "positive valuation of private life," and "the intensity of the relations to self." He maintains the culture of the self in imperial times is not "the manifestation of growing individualism" but the "peak" of a phenomenon of long duration which corresponds to an intensification and a valorization of relations to the self. In a discussion at Berkeley in the spring of 1983, Foucault states that "what happened in the fourth century say, between Socrates and then Epictetus, is not the birth of individualism as is often claimed. In general, the development of Stoicism, the transition from early Stoicism to late Stoicism, is associated with the development of individualism. But I don't think this is individualism, because Epictetus's sage, or without going to that radical extreme, the Stoic sage is someone who is more than others tied into a whole series of obligations to humanity: the sage is a missionary. The portrait of the Cynic offered by Epictetus in the third book of the *Discourses* presents him as a missionary entirely dedicated to others. One couldn't be further from individualism here. On the other hand, I believe the relation to oneself as a condition for the relation to others is a very important element, as is the fact that you can only have a relationship with oth-

ers once you have established a certain relationship to yourself (one in which you exercise full sovereignty over yourself). Rather than leading to the appearance of individualism, it seems to me this development in ancient philosophy tends to develop and intensify the importance of the relationship to oneself." See Discussion with Michel Foucault, D 250 (8), 11–12.

27. Plutarch, "Sayings of Spartans," in *Moralia*, vol. 3, trans. Frank Cole Babbit, Loeb Classical Library (Cambridge, MA: Harvard University Press, 1931), 217A, sect. 3 (p. 297). See *HS*, 31.

28. Xenophon, *The Education of Cyrus*, trans. and annotated Wayne Ambler (Ithaca: Cornell University Press, 2001), book 7, chap. 5, sect. 42 (p. 225). "After they came together, Cyrus said such things as follow to them: 'Men, friends and allies, we cannot possibly blame the gods with the charge that, up to this point, not all we prayed for has been accomplished. If, however, to have great success entails the result that it is not possible to have leisure either for oneself or to enjoy oneself with friends, I bid farewell to this happiness." [This book is titled *The Cyropaedia* in older translations.—Trans.]

29. Plato, *Alcibiades*, trans. D. S. Hutchinson, in *Complete Works*, 557–95. Foucault analyzes Plato's *Alcibiades* in detail from the perspective of the care of the self, in his course at the Collège de France *The Hermeneutics of the Subject*. See *HS*, 32–46, 51–59, 66–78, and passim. See also Foucault, "Technologies of the Self," 225–28. In his Collège de France course *The Courage of Truth*, Foucault designates the *Alcibiades* and the *Laches* as the starting points of two different traditions of care for the self and, more generally, of Western philosophy: "philosophy as that which, by prompting and encouraging men to take care of themselves, leads them to the metaphysical reality of the soul, and, on the other, philosophy as a test of life, a test of existence, and the elaboration of a particular kind of form and modality of life." So we have on the one hand, a philosophy which makes knowledge of the soul or an "ontology of the self" (metaphysical discourse) possible and, on the other, "a philosophy as test of life, of *bios*, which is the ethical material and object of an art of oneself." (an aesthetics of existence). *CT*, 127. See also *CT* 160–62, 236–37.

30. On Albinus, Proclus, and the classification of Plato's work, Fou-

cault refers to the study of André-Jean Festugière, "L'ordre de lecture des dialogues de Platon aux Vᵉ/VIᵉ siècles," in *Études de philosophie grecque* (Paris: Vrin, 1971), 535–50. On the Neoplatonist commentaries on the *Alcibiades*, see *HS*, 170–75.

31. On the salient features of the "care of the self" during the imperial period, see *HS*, 81, 492–96; *CS*, 43–68. Foucault observes a radical difference between the Greco-Roman culture of the self and the contemporary culture of the self, in spite of certain continuities. (This is marked by a veritable "overturning" of the experience of the self which, he sees as produced precisely within Christianity). See "Discussion with the Department of French," this volume, pp. 117–20, reproduced in part in "On the Genealogy of Ethics," 271, and "À propos de la généalogie de l'éthique: Un aperçu du travail en cours," *DE II*, no. 344, 1443.

32. Epicurus, "The Letter to Menoeceus," in *Saint Paul and Epicurus* by Norman Wentworth deWitt (Minneapolis: University of Minnesota Press, 1954), 188–89. "Let no one delay to philosophize while he is young nor weary in philosophizing when he is old, for no one is either short of the age or past the age for enjoying health of the soul. And the man who says the time for philosophizing has not yet come or is already past may be compared to the man who says the time for happiness is not yet come or is already gone by."

33. See this volume, p. 172, n. 18.

34. Galen, *On the Passions and Errors of the Soul*, 37. "For each of us needs almost a lifetime of training to become a perfect man. Indeed, a man must not give up trying to make himself better even if, at the age of fifty, he should see that his soul has suffered damage which is not incurable but which has been left uncorrected."

35. In the inaugural lecture of his Collège de France course *The Hermeneutics of the Subject*, Foucault observes that already in Socrates's *Apology*, in contrast to the *Alcibiades*, the care of the self appears as "a general function of the whole of life." To a certain extent this anticipates the Hellenistic and Roman conception of care for the self as "a permanent obligation for every individual throughout his life." See *HS*, 37–39.

36. In the lecture delivered on February 10, 1982, as part of his Collège de France course *The Hermeneutics of the Subject*, Foucault distinguishes three forms of "conversion": Platonic *epistrophē*, Hellenistic and Roman

conversion, and Christian *metanoia*. See *HS*, 206–17. On the *epistrophē eis heauton* as a "common goal" of practices of the self in imperial times, see also *CS*, 64–67.

37. On the three functions (the critical function, the function of struggle and the therapeutic function) of self-care in imperial times, see *HS*, 93–100, 231–32, 322, 495–96. For the close correlation between care of the self and medical thought and practice, see also *CS*, 54–58.

38. Plutarch, "Advice About Keeping Well," in *Moralia*, vol 2, trans. Frank Cole Babbitt, Loeb Classical Library (Cambridge, MA: Harvard University Press, 1928), 122E (p. 219).

39. Foucault is referring to two passages from Epictetus, *Discourses*: (1) "the lecture-room of the philosopher is a hospital; you ought not to walk out of it in pleasure, but in pain. For you are not well when you come; one man has a dislocated shoulder, another an abscess, another a fistula, another a headache. And then am I to sit down and recite to you dainty little notions and clever little mottoes, so that you will go out with words of praise on your lips, one man carrying away his shoulder just as it was when he came in, another his head in the same state, another his fistula, another his abscess" Epictetus, *Discourses*, books 3–4, *Fragments: The Encheiridion*, trans. W. A. Oldfather, Loeb Classical Library (Cambridge, MA: Harvard University Press, 1928), book 3, chap. 23, sect. 30–32 (p. 181). (2) "If you ask me now, 'Are our syllogisms useful?' I will tell you that they are, and, if you wish, I will show how they are useful. 'Have they, then, helped *me* at all?' Man, you did not ask, did you? whether they are useful to you, but whether they are useful in general? Let the man who is suffering from dysentery ask me whether vinegar is useful; I will tell him that it is useful. 'Is it useful, then, to me?' I will say, 'No. Seek first to have your discharge stopped, the little ulcers healed.' So do you also, men, first cure your ulcers, stop your discharges, be tranquil in mind, bring it free from distraction into the school; and then you will know what power reason has." Epictetus, *Discourses*, book 2, chap. 21, sect. 21–22 (p. 381).

40. Galen, *On the Passions and Errors of the Soul*, 40–41, 54.

41. On the progressive "separation" of the care of the self from the erotic in the history of the Greco-Roman world, see *HS*, 60, 337–38 and *CS*, 189–232. On the Roman exclusion of the love of boys and the transfer of salient features of the pederastic relationship to within marriage,

see *ST*, 181–97. Finally, on the problematization of the relationship between pedagogy and eroticism already present in classical Greece, see *ST*, 92–95.

42. Lucius Annaeus Seneca, "Letter 52, 1–3: Good Learners and Good Teachers," in *Letters on Ethics: To Lucilius*, trans. Margaret Graver and A. A. Long (Chicago: University of Chicago Press, 2015), 149–50. For a more detailed analysis of the theme of *stultitia* in this text as well as in Seneca's *On Tranquility of Mind*, see *HS*, 130–35.

43. On the role of writing in the practice of the self, in particular, *hupomnēmata* and correspondence, see *HS*, 359–62 and Foucault, "Self Writing," in *EW* 1:207–22 (*DE*, no. 329).

44. Aelius Aristides, *Aelius Aristides and the Sacred Tales*, trans. Charles. A. Behr (Amsterdam: A. M. Hakkert, 1968). See Foucault, "Technologies of the Self," 242.

45. See also *HS*, 11–31 on this problem. But here, after talking about the "paradoxes of the history of morality" in response to the same kind of questions, Foucault attributes the responsibility for the philosophical recycling of the *gnōthi seauton* and the exclusion of *epimeleia heautou* to the "Cartesian moment."

46. See *ABHS*, 76. "Maybe the problem of the self is not to discover what it is in its positivity, maybe the problem is not to discover a positive self, or the positive foundation of the self. Maybe our problem is now to discover that the self is nothing else than the historical correlation of the technology built in our history. Maybe the problem is to change those technologies. And in this case, one of the main political problems would be nowadays, in the strict sense of the word, the politics of ourselves." In 1982, in "The Subject and Power," in *EW* 3 (*DE*, no. 306) after having evoked Kant's text on the Aufklärung and the "great philosophical task" which it inaugurated—namely "the critical analysis of our world"—Foucault specifies: "Maybe the target nowadays is not to discover what we are but to refuse what we are. [...] The conclusion would be that the political, ethical, social, philosophical problem of our days is not to try to liberate the individual from the state, and from the state's institutions, but to liberate us both from the state and the type of individualization linked to the state. We have to promote new forms of subjectivity through the refusal of this kind of individuality that has been imposed on us for several centuries" (336, translation modified).

47. Synesius of Cyrene, "On Dreams," in *On Prophecy, Dreams and Human Imagination: Synesius, De Insommniis*, trans. Donald A. Russell (Tübingen: Mohr Siebeck, 2014), 12–59. See Foucault, "Rêver de ses plaisirs. Sur l''Onirocritique' d'Artémidore," in *DE II*, no. 332, 1283; "On the Genealogy of Ethics," 275; "Technologies of the Self," 242; *CS*, 5–6.

48. Epicurus, "The Letter to Menoeceus," 188–89. See this volume, p. 175, n. 32.

49. The question alludes to a passage from book 6 of Jacques Lacan's seminar dedicated to Hamlet. A lengthy extract was published in the United States in 1977 under the title "Desire and Interpretation of Desire in Hamlet," *Yale French Studies* 55/56 (1977): 11–52. See Jacques Lacan, *Desire and its Interpretation*, trans. Bruce Fink, book 6 of *The Seminar of Jacques Lacan*, ed. Jacques Alain-Miller (London: Polity Press, 2019).

50. On the importance for the Greeks, of determining the opportune time, *kairos*, and on the role of this notion in ancient ethics particularly in relation to the art of making use of pleasures, see *UP*, 57–59, and *CS*, 130–31. In the lecture delivered on March 10, 1982, as part of his course at the Collège de France *The Hermeneutics of the Subject*, Foucault highlights the importance of this notion in the practice of *parrēsia*. See *HS*, 384–85, 388.

51. Plutarch, "Table Talk 3, Question 6," in *Moralia*, vol. 8, trans. P. A. Clement, H. B. Hoffleit, Loeb Classical Library (Cambridge, MA: Harvard University Press, 1969), 653B–655D (pp. 243–57).

52. On the notion of "crisis" in ancient medical thought and practice, see *PP*, 242–45.

53. See Michel Foucault, "Interview de Michel Foucault (entretien avec J. F.et J. de Wit)," in *DE II*, no. 349, 1484: "Psychoanalysis is therefore principally a science, it's a technique of work on the self, founded on confession." [A version of this interview has been translated into English. Michel Foucault, "Interview with Jean François and John de Wit," in *WDTT*, 253–69. The editors note (p. 8) that this translation is based on the typescript of a lost audio recording, adding: "this version differs from the version published in *Dits et Écrits*, which consisted of a French translation of a Dutch adaptation of the interview (which had itself been translated from French into Dutch and published in a Dutch journal.)"—Trans.]

54. On this definition of ethics, see Foucault, "On the Genealogy of

Ethics," 263, and *UP*, 26–28, 251. On ethics as a "relation to oneself," see also Foucault, "On the Genealogy of Ethics," 266, and "À propos de la généalogie de l'éthique," 620.

55. Epictetus, *Discourses*, book 3, chap. 23, sect. 30–32 (p. 181). See this volume, p. 176, n. 39. See *HS*, 99, 336–37, 496; *CS*, 55.

56. See *ABHS*, 75. In an interview conducted at the end of 1981, Foucault says that "The art of living means killing psychology, and creating unnameable individualities, beings, relationships, and qualities within oneself and with others." See Michel Foucault, "Werner Schroeter and Michel Foucault in Conversation," in Michel Foucault, Patrice Maniglier, and Dork Zabunyan, *Foucault at the Movies*, ed. and trans. Clare O'Farrell (New York: Columbia University Press, 2018), 185 (*DE*, no. 308).

57. See for example Epictetus, *Discourses*, book 3, chap. 3, sect. 14–22 (pp. 33–35) with the description of the "stroll-exercise," to which Foucault returns several times. He specifically emphasizes the operation of division and sorting that needs to be applied to the different representations the world excites in us. This is so we can define to what extent these representations depend or don't depend on us, and thus establish "the attitude to adopt towards them." See *HS*, 298–99. See also *HS*, 241, 503–4; "Technologies of the Self," 241; this volume, p. 132, reproduced in part in "On the Genealogy of Ethics," 27, and in "À propos de la généalogie de l'éthique," 1447.

58. Cassian is referring to the abbot John of Lycon. See John Cassian, "First Conference: On the Goal and the End of the Monk," in *The Conferences*, trans. and annotated Boniface Ramsey, Ancient Christian Writers 57 (New York: Paulist Press, 1997), chap. 21, sect. 1 (p. 85). On this anecdote see *GL*, 291, 294–95, 302.

59. See *ABHS*, 68, nn. 69–70.

60. In a discussion with Hubert Dreyfus and Paul Rabinow at Berkeley in April 1983, Foucault explains: "In fact, I don't think you find this idea of an illusion about yourself in pagan antiquity. You can be ignorant about yourself, that's a very old Socratic theme. And as Charles Taylor puts it very clearly [...] the Stoic problem is 'Who am I?' But the answer is to be found in the delimitation between what is dependent on me and what is not dependent on me. And I think this ignorance about what is dependent on me and what is not dependent is a different thing from illusions about myself when I am not able to know, or to recognize

if a desire I have or an idea I have, comes from my mind, comes from God or from the Devil. So that's a change, and a very important one." See Discussion with Michel Foucault, D 250 (5), p. 15.

61. See *ABHS*, 116, and "'Foucault' by Maurice Florence," 461.

62. On the notion of *gnōmē*, which is at the same time a form of knowledge, a precept, a truth, and a rule, see *ABHS*, 36–38 as well as *WDTT*, 132–33. See also *ABHS*, 49–50, n. 35.

63. On the role of memory in the ancient world particularly in Platonic philosophy, see *HS*, 176, 325–26, 455–66, 460–61.

64. Christopher Lasch, *The Culture of Narcissism: American Life in an Age of Diminishing Expectations* (New York: W. W. Norton, 1979).

65. See Michel Foucault, "Sexuality and Power," in *Religion and Culture*, ed. Jeremy Carrette, trans. Richard A. Lynch (Manchester: Manchester University Press, 1999), 120–21 (*DE*, no. 233), and "Preface to *The History of Sexuality*, Volume Two," 204–5. In the first volume of *The History of Sexuality*, Foucault describes two correlative processes that have developed in the West regarding the "question" of sex: "we demand that sex speak the truth" and "we demand that it tell us our truth, or rather, the deeply buried truth of that truth about ourselves which we think we possess in immediate consciousness." In his view, this is how "there has evolved over several centuries, a knowledge of the subject." See *HIST*, 69–70. But by going back in time, Foucault discovered forms of the constitution of the relation to self through sexual experience that were profoundly different to this modern form. He explores this notably in his course at the Collège de France *Subjectivity and Truth*, as well as in the last two volumes of *The History of Sexuality*. And as he explained in his 1980 lectures *About the Beginning of the Hermeneutics of the Self*, it was precisely by studying the experience of sexuality that he was able to observe the existence of "techniques of the self" across all societies. See *ABHS*, 25.

66. On the Greek problematization of the man-boy sexual relationship, and on the "desexualization" of pedagogical erotics, see *ST*, 92–95. See also Foucault, "The Concern for Truth," 458; and *UP*, 19–20.

67. On this subject, see among other works *DP*, 177–84, 296–308; Foucault, "About the Concept of the 'Dangerous Individual' in Nineteenth-Century Legal Psychiatry," in *EW* 3:176–200 (*DE*, no. 220); *WDTT*, 211–29.

68. Michel Foucault, "Nietzsche, Genealogy, History," in *EW* 2:368–91 (*DE*, no. 84).

69. See this volume, pp. 163–65, nn. 30 and 32. In his 1984 article on Kant and the Aufklärung published in the United States, Foucault states critique is "genealogical in its finality and archaeological in its method." (See Foucault, "What Is Enlightenment?," 315.) Foucault had already previously proposed this framework of archaeology-method and genealogy-goal in 1980 in the Howison Lectures at Berkeley, where he explained that "In sum, the aim of my project is to construct a genealogy of the subject" and that "the method is an archaeology of knowledge." See *ABHS*, 23, n. b. See also Foucault, this volume, p. 100.

70. See this volume, p. 171, n. 11.

71. On the continuity of the "codifying framework" of sexual ethics, from imperial times through Christianity to the present day see *ST*, 230–33, 253–55.

72. See Michel Foucault, "The Order of Discourse," ed. Nancy Luxon, trans. Thomas Scott-Railton, in *Archives of Infamy: Foucault on State Power in the Lives of Ordinary Citizens* (Minneapolis: University of Minnesota Press, 2019), 153–54. "Within its limits, each discipline recognizes true and false propositions, but it also rejects beyond its margins, a whole teratology of knowledge-*savoir*. [...] [A] proposition must fulfill complex and weighty requirements to be able to belong to the ensemble of a discipline; before being called true or false, it must be, as Monsieur Canguilhem would say, 'in the truth' ['*dans le vrai*']."

73. Thomas S. Kuhn, *The Structure of Scientific Revolutions* (Chicago: University of Chicago Press, 1962).

74. Michel Foucault, *The Order of Things: An Archaeology of the Human Sciences*, (London: Tavistock Publications, 1970).

75. Michel Foucault, *History of Madness*, trans. Jonathan Murphy and Jean Khalfa (London: Routledge, 2006 [1961]).

76. See Michel Foucault, "The Politics of Health in the Eighteenth Century," in *EW* 3:90–105 (*DE*, no. 168); "The Birth of Social Medicine," in *EW* 3:134–56 (*DE*, no. 196); "The Politics of Health in the Eighteenth Century," trans. Richard A. Lynch, *Foucault Studies* 18 (2014): 113–27, (*DE*, no. 257).

77. In the second version of "The Politics of Health in the Eighteenth Century," 124–27, Foucault cites several books in French and German, a

list that might include the two works he is alluding to here. See in particular Johann Peter Frank, *System einer vollständigen medicinischen Polizey,* 4 vols. (Mannheim: C. F. Schwan, 1779–1790); abridged and translated into English as *A System of Complete Medical Police: Selections from Johann Peter Frank,* ed. Erna Lesky (Baltimore: Johns Hopkins University Press, 1976). See also the first version: "The Politics of Health in the Eighteenth Century," 95; "The Birth of Social Medicine," 140; "The Political Technology of Individuals," 404–5.

78. This student was Blandine Barret-Kriegel, who would later publish a four-volume history based on this work, *Les historiens et la monarchie,* 4 vols. (Paris: Presses Universitaires de France, 1988). This work was republished by Presses Universitaires de France in 1996 under the more Foucauldian title *L'Histoire à l'âge classique.*

79. On the birth of historico-political discourse, see Michel Foucault, *"Society Must Be Defended": Lectures at the Collège de France, 1975–1976,* ed. M. Bertani and A. Fontana, trans. David Macey, English series editor Arnold I. Davidson (New York: Picador, 2003), 48–62.

80. See *DP,* 114–31.

81. See *DP,* 135–94, 227–28, 302–3. See also Michel Foucault, *The Punitive Society: Lectures at the Collège de France, 1972–1973,* ed. Bernard E. Harcourt, trans. Graham Burchell, English series ed. Arnold I. Davidson (New York and Basingstoke: Palgrave Macmillan, 2015), 239–41.

82. See *DP,* 200–209. See also *PP,* 41, 73–79.

83. Erving Goffman (1922–1982). On the notion of the "total institution," see Goffman, *Asylums: Essays on the Social Situation of Mental Patients and Other Inmates* (New York, Doubleday, 1961).

84. This is why in the discussion that followed the Howison Lectures at Berkely Foucault clearly asserted that "it's not possible to find any hermeneutics of the self in Plato." Plato's problem, is actually "the elevation of the soul towards truth; it's not to find the truth in the depths of the soul." See Foucault, "Debate on 'Truth and subjectivity,'" in *ABHS,* 111. On this kind of "ontological knowledge of oneself as a soul," in Plato, see also this volume, pp. 130–31, and *CT,* 127–28.

85. On the Stoics' "meditation" or "exercise" of death, see *HS,* 477–80, 504.

86. See Seneca, "Letter 12, 6–9: Visiting a Childhood Home," in *Letters on Ethics,* 49–50.

87. Lucius Annaeus Seneca, "On Anger," in *Anger, Mercy, Revenge,* trans. Robert A. Kaster (Chicago: University of Chicago Press, 2010), book 3, chap. 36, sect. 1–3 (p. 91). For Foucault's commentary on this text, see *GL,* 239–46; *ABHS,* 30–33; *WDTT,* 97–100; *HS,* 162–63, 481–85; Foucault, "Technologies of the Self," 244–46; *Fearless Speech,* ed. J. Pearson (Los Angeles: Semiotext(e), 2001), 145–50; *CS,* 59–62.

88. The treatise *Peri euthumias (On Tranquility of Mind)* is actually addressed to a certain Paccius, but Fundanus is mentioned at the beginning of this treatise, which is likewise the case in another treatise by Plutarch entitled *Peri aorgēsias (De cohibenda ira)* ("On the Control of Anger"). In the lecture delivered on March 3, 1982, in his Collège de France course *The Hermeneutics of the Subject,* Foucault refers to *Peri euthumias,* specifying that "Plutarch replies to one of his correspondents, Paccius." See *HS,* 362.

89. See Plutarch, "On Tranquility of Mind," in *Moralia,* vol. 6, 464E–F (p. 167).

90. On the evolution and characteristics of Christian confession from the thirteenth century onwards, and particularly on Canon XXI of the Fourth Lateran Council of 1215 regulating the sacrament of penance, see *AB,* 174–93; and *WDTT,* 184–91.

91. On the theme of the "aesthetics of existence," see among other references, Foucault, "On the Genealogy of Ethics," 255, 260–61, 264, 274, 278; "Rêver de ses plaisirs," 1307; "À propos de la généalogie de l'éthique," 1429–30, 1434; "An Aesthetics of Existence," in *FL,* 451 (*DE,* no. 357); *CT,* 161–65; *UP,* 89–92.

92. On the strategic importance, not just of talking about, but in *creating* pleasure and new possibilities for pleasure, see "Michel Foucault: An Interview by Stephen Riggins," in *EW* 1:131 (*DE,* no. 336); and "Sex, Power and the Politics of Identity," in *FL,* 384–85 (*DE,* no. 358): "Pleasure also must be part of our culture. It is very interesting to note, for instance, that for centuries people generally, as well as doctors, psychiatrists and even liberation movements, have always spoken about desire, and never about pleasure. 'We have to release our desire,' they say. No! We have to create new pleasure. Then maybe desire will follow." See also Michel Foucault, "Sexualité et politique" (entretien avec C. Nemoto et M. Watanabe), *DE II,* no. 230, p. 527.

93. In the lecture delivered on March 11, 1981, in his course at the

Collège de France *Subjectivity and Truth*, Foucault argues that "the great Western problematic of desire arises within the ideal image of the conjugal family and of the relation between man and wife as defined at that moment." This took place in the Roman world of the first century AD. See *ST*, 217–19. On the constitution of the "subject of desire," see also *ST*, 286–89, and *UP*, 5–6.

94. R. H. van Gulik, *Sexual Life in Ancient China: A Preliminary Survey of Chinese Sex and Society from ca. 1500 B.C. till 1644* (Leiden: Brill, 2021 [1961]). See Foucault, "À propos de la généalogie de l'éthique," 1441, and *UP*, 137.

95. Foucault notes that in the "erotic arts" (*ars erotica*)—in "China, Japan, India, Rome, in Arabo-Moslem societies [. . .] truth is drawn from pleasure itself, understood as a practice and accumulated as experience," in direct opposition to what he terms "the science of sex" (*scientia sexualis*). See *HIST*, 57–63; "The West and the Truth of Sex," trans. Lawrence Winters, *Sub-Stance* 6/7, no. 20 (1978): 7 (*DE*, no. 181); "Sexuality and Power," in *Religion and Culture*, ed. Jeremy Carrette, trans. Richard A. Lynch (Manchester: Manchester University Press, 1999), 119 (*DE*, no. 233). In a 1983 interview, however, Foucault specifies that "the Greeks and Romans did not have any *ars erotica* to be compared with the Chinese *ars erotica* [. . .]. They had a *tekhnē tou biou* in which the economy of pleasure played a very large role. See Foucault, "On the Genealogy of Ethics," 259, and "À propos de la généalogie de l'éthique," 1434.

96. In a discussion at Berkeley in April 1983, Foucault says that his "problem is why do we think that it's not possible to have sexual ethics without the obligation of knowing, deciphering, discovering, disclosing, and telling the truth about ourselves? That's the link between sexual ethics and the truth of the self which is my genealogical problem." See Discussion with Michel Foucault, D 250 (5), p. 14.

97. Foucault uses the French pronunciation of the word. On the Christian notion of concupiscence, see *AB*, 184–94, 201–27; and Foucault, "The Battle for Chastity," in *EW* 1:185–97 (*DE*, no. 312).

98. A number of Foucault's responses in this debate were taken up and reused by Hubert Dreyfus and Paul Rabinow—most often by cutting, regrouping, or reformulating them—in order to "construct" the in-

terview "On the Genealogy of Ethics," published in English in 1983 (see
EW 1:253–80) and in French in 1984 with a number of modifications
made by Foucault himself (see Foucault, "A propos de la généalogie de
l'éthique," 1428–50).

99. See this volume, p. 183, n. 91.

100. In the lectures titled *About the Beginning of the Hermeneutics of
the Self*, Foucault describes this "reversal" in terms of the passage from
the "gnomic self," which is "not to be discovered but to be constituted
through the force of truth," to the "gnoseological self," which on the
contrary is "like a text or like a book that we have to decipher" by her-
meneutical work, so as to better renounce ourselves. See *ABHS*, 36–37,
77. See also *GL*, 294–304, and *WDTT*, 91–94, 141–51, 163–68.

101. See this volume, pp. 80–81 and 177, n. 43.

102. Plato, *Phaedrus*, trans. Alexander Nehamas and Paul Woodruff,
in *Complete Works*, 274c–275e (pp. 551–52).

103. Xenophon, "Memorabilia," in *Memorabilia, Oeconomicus, Sym-
posium, Apology*, trans. E. C. Marchant and O. J. Todd, revised by Jeffrey
Henderson, Loeb Classical Library (Cambridge, MA: Harvard University Press, 2013), book 4, chap. 8, sect. 9 (p. 369).

104. Foucault had already previously used this expression in 1980 in
the conclusion to his lectures *About the Beginning of the Hermeneutics
of the Self* but in a slightly different sense. Rather than referring to the
problem of the government of the self or establishing a "political" type
of relationship to oneself, it referred to the problem of the technologies
that have manufactured our "self" in the course of our history. These
technologies needed to be changed in Foucault's view. It was a task
he saw as strictly political. See *ABHS*, 76, 78. Also, in a discussion at
Berkeley, in April 1983, Foucault specified that, even if on occasion, "in
ancient ethics, people sought to define their own relation to themselves
as a relation of power," for all this, the relation to oneself "is not a relation of power." The relationship of "mastery" one has with oneself
must therefore be distinguished from power relations with others. See
Discussion with Michel Foucault, D 250 (9), 17.

105. See Foucault, "Self Writing," 207–22.

106. Seneca, "Letter 55: Passing the Home of a Recluse," in *Letters on
Ethics*, 157–59. See Foucault, "Self Writing," 218.

107. In actuality, the letters of Cicero and Seneca are separated by almost a century.

108. Athanasius of Alexandria, "Life of St. Anthony of Egypt," in *Medieval Hagiography: An Anthology*, ed. Thomas Head, trans. David Brakke (London: Routledge, 2001), chap. 55 (pp. 19–20). See *GL*, 257; *WDTT*, 144–45; Foucault, "Self Writing," 208–14.

109. On Artemidorus's *Oneirocritica*, see Foucault, "Sexuality and Solitude," 180; *ST*, 47–69; "Rêver de ses plaisirs," 1281–1307; *CS*, 4–36.

110. See Synesius of Cyrene, *On Dreams*, 18, 20 (pp. 51–52, 55–57). See this volume, p. 178, n. 47.

111. Synesius of Cyrene (ca. AD 370–414) lived after the death of Saint Anthony (ca. AD 251–356).

112. See this volume, p. 180, n. 62.

113. Seneca, "Letter 55: Passing the Home of a Recluse," in *Letters on Ethics*, 157–59.

114. Demetrius, *On Style*, in *Aristotle: On Poetics; Longinus: On the Sublime; Demetrius: On Style*, ed. and trans. S. Halliwell, trans. D. Russell, W. H. Fyfe, D. C. Innes, and W. Rhys Roberts, Loeb Classical Library (Cambridge, MA: Harvard University Press, 1995), 309–521. The attribution of this treatise to Demetrius of Phalerum (350–282 BC) is doubtful; it is probably later. See Foucault, "Self Writing," 215–17.

115. Seneca, "Letter 75.1: What it Means to Make Progress," in *Letters on Ethics*, 236. "You complain that I am expending less care on the letters I send you. So I am, for who expends care over a conversation? Only one who deliberately adopts an affected manner of speaking. I wish my letters to be like what my conversation would be if you and I were sitting or walking together: easy and unstudied. They have in them nothing forced, nothing feigned." For a more detailed commentary on this letter, in relation to Foucault's analysis of *parrēsia* in the context of ancient direction of conscience, see *HS*, 401–7, and Foucault, "Parrēsia," *Critical Inquiry* 41, no. 2 (2015): 219–53.

116. Plato, *Phaedrus*, 276a–277c (pp. 552–54).

117. Foucault is probably referring to the dematerialization of shares and bonds which became effective in France from 1984.

118. On these complex relationships, see *HS*, 2–15, 440–43.

119. Plato, *Alcibiades*, 127d–130e (pp. 585–89).

120. *HS*, 66–69.

121. Plato, *Alcibiades*, 132d–33c (pp. 591–92). See *HS*, 69–70, and this volume, p. 106 and p. 182, n. 84.

122. Foucault says "Pythagoreans," but given the context, this was probably more a practice engaged in by the Epicurean groups reported by Philodemus (a practice which is indeed of Pythagorean origin).

123. On Philodemus and the Epicurean practice of the examination and direction of conscience (coupled with the theme of *parrēsia*), see *HS*, 137, 387–91; *CS*, 51–52.

124. On the practice of self-examination in antiquity, see *GL*, 235–46; *ABHS*, 27–32; *WDTT*, 93–102; *HS*, 462–64, 480–85; Foucault, "Self Writing," 219–21; "Technologies of the Self," 235–38; *CS*, 50–51, 60–64.

125. Epictetus, *Discourses*, book 3, chap. 3, sect. 14–22 (pp. 33–35). See this volume, p. 179, n. 57.

126. *The Meditations of the Emperor Marcus Aurelius Antoninus*, ed. James Moore and Michael Silverthorne, trans. Francis Hutcheson and James Moore, Natural Law and Enlightenment Classics (Liberty Fund, 2007), book 4, chap. 3 (pp. 47–48). See *HS*, 50, 500.

127. *Hamartēmata*: errors, faults.

128. Foucault mounts a similar argument in the Howison Lectures at Berkeley in his analysis of the beginning of Seneca's *De tranquillitate* (*On Tranquility of Mind*) and his explanation of the meaning of Serenus's *verum fateri* (truth telling). He says, "For him it is a question of indicating, as exactly as possible, to what he is still attached and from what he is already detached, in what respect he is free and on what external things he is dependent." His "confession" therefore, "is not the bringing into the light of day of profound secrets. It is rather in terms of the ties which attached him to things of which he is not the master. It is a kind of inventory of freedom in the frame of a code of actions. It is not an enumeration of past faults, it is a balance sheet of dependences." See *ABHS*, 34, n. a.

129. In his lectures *About the Beginning of the Hermeneutics of the Self*, Foucault analyzes the evening examination Seneca describes in the third book of *On Anger*, but also relocates it alongside other Stoic exercises (continual reading of the manual of precepts, the *praemeditatio malorum*, the morning list of tasks that needed to be done and so on). Fou-

cault says that "the self, in all those exercises is not considered as a field of subjective data which have to be interpreted" (as in Christianity): "It submits itself to the trial of possible or real action." See *ABHS*, 32.

130. Ignatius of Loyola, *The Spiritual Exercises of St. Ignatius: Translation Based on Studies in the Language of the Autograph*, trans. Louis J. Puhl (Chicago: Loyola Press, 2021).

131. Foucault mounts a similar argument elsewhere, adding techniques of signification alongside techniques of production, power, and the self. See *ABHS*, 24–25; Foucault, "Sexuality and Solitude," 177; "Technologies of the Self," 225.

132. In an interview conducted in Japan in 1978 (and before forming the concept of "techniques of the self"), Foucault claimed that the techniques of Buddhist spirituality "tend toward [. . .] deindividualisation, desubjectivization, in effect to push individuality to its limits and beyond its limits in order to liberate the subject." Foucault, "The Philosophical Scene: Foucault Interviewed by Moriaki Watanabe," 236. See also Foucault, "Michel Foucault and Zen: A Stay in a Zen Temple," 112.

133. The question refers to Ruth Benedict's distinction between shame cultures and guilt cultures. This distinction was taken up by Eric R. Dodds in his analysis of the evolution of the ancient Greek world from the Homeric period to the classical period. See Eric R. Dodds, *The Greeks and the Irrational* (Oakland: University of California Press, 2020 [1951]), 17, 28–63.

134. Ramsay MacMullen, *Roman Social Relations, 50 B.C. to A.D. 284* (New Haven: Yale University Press, 1974). Actually, MacMullen's position is more nuanced. See p. 109 concerning Imperial Roman society: "What anthropologists would call a 'shame society' was of course a 'pride society' too."

135. See this volume, p. 157, n. 8.

136. Jacob Burckhardt, *The Civilization of the Renaissance in Italy* (London: Phaidon, 1995 [1860]). See *UP*, 11.

137. For the distinction, within "morality," in the broad sense between "codes of behavior" and "forms of moral subjectivation and the practices of self that are meant to ensure it," see *UP*, 29. See also *ST*, 230–32 where Foucault opposes "the codifying framework that [determines] the permitted and the prohibited" to "these accompanying discourses"

which "are not just the theoretical garment of a codification" because it is due to this that it is possible to grasp "the type of relationship that there may be between subjectivity [and] the codification of conducts."

138. On knowledge of the world and nature as an exercise of the self, see *HS*, 243, 258–311. See also Pierre Hadot, "Physics as a Spiritual Exercise, or Pessimism and Optimism in Marcus Aurelius" in *The Selected Writings of Pierre Hadot: Philosophy as Practice*, trans. Matthew Sharpe and Federico Testa (London: Bloomsbury, 2020), 207–26. In a discussion at Berkeley in spring 1983, Foucault says: "I think we need to make some adjustments to what's been said about the cosmos in Stoicism and in general in ancient philosophy. This is because there's a theme that is curiously recurrent and present in all of ancient philosophy from Socrates to Epictetus. This is that we don't need to know all those useless things concerning astronomy, non-medicinal plants and what happens in the bottom of the sea. You find all this nonstop: Plato and Aristotle are exceptions. They are not typical representatives of ancient thought at all, they are monsters in ancient thought, where you perpetually find the theme that you only have to deal with things that are directly useful to existence. It is in Socrates, in all of late Stoicism, it is in Epictetus and Epicurus. So, this relation to the cosmos which is indeed present, is very significantly marked by the importance of the relation to the self." See Discussion with Michel Foucault, D 250 (8), 13.

139. On the "Cartesian moment" as the moment in the history of truth when "knowledge itself and knowledge alone gives access to the truth," see *HS*, 14, 17.

140. In the inaugural lecture of his course at the Collège de France *The Hermeneutics of the Subject*, Foucault draws a distinction between philosophy ("the form of thought that asks what it is that enables the subject to have access to the truth and which attempts to determine the conditions and limits of the subject's access to the truth") and "spirituality." The latter is understood as "the set of these researches, practices, and experiences, which may be purifications, ascetic exercises, renunciations, conversions of looking, modifications of existence, etc." that constitute for the subject "the price to be paid for access to the truth." Foucault claims that, throughout antiquity, the philosophical question and the practice of spirituality "were never separate." See *HS*, 15, 17.

141. On alchemical knowledge and its complex relationship to "scientific" thought, see *PP*, 241; Foucault, "La maison des fous," in *DE I*, no. 146, 1562–63; *HS*, 27.

142. See this volume, p. 189, n. 139.

143. In his course at the Collège de France *The Hermeneutics of the Subject*, after discussing Descartes and the constitution of a subject which, "as such became capable of truth," Foucault argues that "the supplementary twist" can be found in Kant. In this instance, however, he is referring to the *Critique of Pure Reason*. This "consists in saying that what we cannot know is precisely the structure itself of the knowing subject, which means that we cannot know the subject. Consequently, the idea of a certain spiritual transformation of the subject, which finally gives him access to something to which precisely he does not have access at that moment, is chimerical and paradoxical. So, the liquidation of what could be called the condition of spirituality for access to the truth is produced with Descartes and Kant; Kant and Descartes seem to me to be the two major moments." See *HS*, 190. In a discussion at Berkeley in spring 1983, Foucault explains that his problem is seeing how "through the forms of relationship with oneself that are proposed, suggested and programmed by techniques of the self, we lead individuals to constitute themselves and to recognize themselves and act as moral subjects." In addition, "when Kant defined the moral subject as being a universal subject, he basically did nothing more than provide one possible formula for this organization and this constitution of the moral subject." Foucault further specifies that, "for a Stoic, or for someone, let's say, in the first two centuries AD, constituting oneself as a moral subject, being a moral subject, meant being an absolutely independent subject in the sense of being a master of oneself. From the moment a person exercised total sovereignty over themselves and did what they did they became a moral subject. This is a formula that is close, but still quite different, from the Kantian formula of universality." See Discussion with Michel Foucault, D 250 (8), 10–11.

144. See Foucault, in this volume, p. 89, and, p. 180, n. 61.

145. In the second hour of the lecture delivered on February 29, 1984, in his course at the Collège de France *The Courage of Truth*, Foucault briefly studies nineteenth- and twentieth-century revolutionary movements in Europe in terms of "support of the Cynic mode of being, of

Cynicism understood as a form of life in the scandal of truth." Revolution, he says, "was not just a political project, it was also a form of life." He proposes the word "militantism" in this context as a description of the "way in which life as revolutionary activity, was defined, described, organized and regulated." This took three major forms: secret societies, trade union organizations or political parties, and "bearing witness by one's life." See *CT*, 183–84.

146. C. Martha, *Les moralistes sous l'Empire romain, philosophes et poètes* (Paris: Hachette, 1865).

147. In his Collège de France course *The Courage of Truth*, while discussing "militancy as bearing witness by one's life in the form of a style of existence," as one of the elements that may have perpetuated the Cynics' theme of true life as an other life in European history Foucault also mentions Dostoevsky and Russian nihilism. See *CT*, 184–85.

148. Jean-Paul Sartre, *Notebooks for an Ethics*, trans. David Pellauer (Chicago: University of Chicago Press, 1992).

INDEX

Abelard, Peter, 145
Aelius Aristides 80–81, 177
Agulhon, Maurice, 160
Albinus, 72, 174
Alcibiades, 15, 72–76, 78, 106, 130, 174, 175, 187
Anthony the Great, 125–27, 186
Aristotle, 70, 186, 189
Arrian, 79
Artemidorus, 126, 186
Athanasius of Alexandria, 125, 127, 186
Augustine of Hippo, 65, 83

Bachelard, Gaston, 3, 34, 151, 168
Barret-Kriegel, Blandine, 182
Bayle, Pierre, 25
Benedict, Ruth, 188
Benedict of Nursia (or Saint Benedict), 108
Bentham, Jeremy, 103–4
Bertani, Mauro, 182
Bichat, Marie François Xavier, 97, 100

Birault, Henri, 50–52, 60
Bonaparte, Napoleon, 66
Bruch, Jean-Louis, 55
Burckhardt, Jacob, 139, 188

Canguilhem, Georges, 1, 3, 34, 149, 158–60, 167, 168, 181
Cassian, John, 88, 179
Cavaillès, Jean, 3, 34, 168
Cicero, 89, 125, 186
Comte, Auguste, 57, 66
Cyrus the Great, 72–73, 174

Defert, Daniel, xi, 149, 156
Demetrius of Phalerum, 128, 186
Descartes, René, 17, 65, 141, 143, 155, 167, 168, 190
Dio of Prusa (or Dio Chrysostom), 69, 74, 172
Dodds, Eric R., 188
Dostoevsky, Fyodor, 191
Dreyfus, Hubert, 162, 171, 179, 184
Dubouchet, Jeanne, 61

Epictetus, 69, 74–77, 79, 86, 131, 132, 135, 136, 172, 173, 176, 179, 187, 189

Epicurus, 75, 84, 175, 178, 189

Evagrius Ponticus, 123

Festugière, André-Jean, 175

Fichte, Johann Gottlieb, 65–66, 147, 169

Finas, Lucette, 161

Fontana, Alessandro, 182

Frank, Johann Peter, 182

Frederick II of Prussia (or Frederick the Great), 29

Fronto, 80, 89

Fundanus, Gaius Minicius, 109–10, 183

Galen (or Claudius Galenus), 69, 74–75, 78, 172, 175, 176

Goffman, Erving, 104, 182

Gouhier, Henri, 1, 48, 54, 55, 58, 61

Gregory of Nyssa, 14, 68–70, 172

Habermas, Jürgen, 39, 54

Hadji-Dimou, Pierre, 58

Hadot, Pierre, 189

Hegel, Georg Wilhelm Friedrich, 34, 65, 168, 170

Heidegger, Martin, 55, 169

Hermotimus, 63, 166

Hesiod, 127

Hobbes, Thomas, 65, 168

Hume, David, 168

Husserl, Edmund, 32, 34, 66, 160

Ignatius of Loyola, 135, 188

John of Lycon, 88, 179

Jolly, Édouard, 150

Kant, Immanuel, 1–7, 9–14, 17, 20, 21, 26, 28–31, 34, 38–39, 48–50, 55, 58–60, 64–66, 112, 143–44, 149–52, 158–61, 163–70, 173, 177, 181, 190

Kirchheimer, Otto, 168

Koyré, Alexandre, 3, 168

Kuhn, Thomas S., 98, 181

Lacan, Jacques, 84–86, 120–21, 178

Laennec, René, 97

Lasch, Christopher, 91, 180

Leibniz, Gottfried Wilhelm, 65, 164, 168

Louis XIV, 101

Lucian of Samosata, 63, 166

Lucilius, 75, 90, 128, 177

Lycinus, 63

MacMullen, Ramsay, 138, 188

Marcus Aurelius, 74, 75, 80, 89, 127, 132, 187, 189

Martha, Constant, 146, 191

Mendel, Gregor, 98–99

Mendelssohn, Moses, 34, 59, 60, 64, 159, 166

Montaigne, Michel de, 126–27, 134–35, 141–42, 147

Mouloud, Noël, 48, 52–53

Musonius Rufus, 69, 75, 172

Nemoto, C., 156, 183

Nietzsche, Friedrich, 34, 66, 95, 139–40, 150, 155, 164–66, 168

Origen, 145

Paccius, 183
Parmenides of Elea, 70
Pascal, Blaise, 141–42
Perrot, Michelle, 160
Philodemus of Gadara, 131, 187
Pindar, 127
Plato, 15, 57, 65, 68, 70, 72, 74, 78,
    105–6, 123, 129–32, 143, 145, 155,
    165, 171, 172, 174, 182, 185–86,
    187, 189
Pliny the Younger, 80
Plutarch, 71, 74–77, 85, 109, 172,
    174, 176, 178, 183
Popper, Karl, 50, 52
Proclus, 72, 174
Protagoras, 58, 165

Rabinow, Paul, 111, 154, 163, 171,
    179, 184
Riggins, Stephen, 92
Rousseau, Jean-Jacques, 60

Sabot, Philippe, 150
Sartre, Jean-Paul, 147, 160, 191
Satan, 88, 125
Schopenhauer, Arthur, 165
Schroeter, Werner, 179

Seneca, 69, 74–76, 79, 80, 89, 90,
    106, 108, 109, 125, 128, 177, 182,
    183, 185–87
Serenus, 78, 187
Sernin, André, 57
Socrates, 14, 54, 55, 58, 68, 69,
    72–75, 78, 122, 130, 132, 152,
    171–73, 175, 189
Spinoza, Baruch, 65, 168
Synesius of Cyrene, 83, 126, 178,
    186

Taylor, Charles, 179

Van Gulik, Robert, 114, 184
Vries, Hans Vredeman de, 98–99

Watanabe, Moriaki, 156, 183, 188
Weber, Max, 35, 66, 38
Wit, Jean François de, 178
Wit, John de, 178
Wycliffe, John, 25

Xenophon, 71–72, 118, 122, 126,
    129–31, 174, 185

Yoshimoto, R., 156

Zac, Sylvain, 58–60